A
Coastal
Affair

By Steve Aikenhead and Peter Seed

The South West Coast Path

How we traveled the Path in five years:

1. Minehead (start)
2. Boscastle
3. Land's End
4. Mevagissey
5. Torquay
6. South Haven Point

A Coastal Affair

Walking England's
South West Coast Path

Steve Aikenhead   Peter Seed

WALK ENGLAND BOOKS

First Edition
Copyright © 2003
Walk England Books
P.O. Box 265
Perkinsville, VT 05151
USA

The authors have made every effort to be
accurate, but cannot assume liability for any
errors. We welcome comments and correc-
tions. Please send them to Steve Aikenhead
at the address for Walk England Books, or
to steve@vermontel.net.

Manufactured in Hong Kong by Colorprint
Offset; New York, Hong Kong, and London

ISBN: 0-9741086-1-8

Cover photograph: from Hartland Quay,
looking north to Hartland Point.
Back cover: Nanjizal Bay, near Land's End.
First title page: near Lynmouth.
Full title page: near Bude.
Right: steps to Polperro on the Coast Path.
Opposite page: near Zennor.
Photo credits: page 192.

THANKS

The South West Coast Path Association exists so that people will have a good Coast Path experience. It is a superb organization, nonprofit and run almost entirely by volunteers. Honorary Secretary Eric Wallis has given a staggering number of hours in helping us with this book and another extremely generous sum of time in helping us along the trail. We thank him warmly and also Lizzie Wallis, the kind and helpful administrator of the SWCPA.

Our friend and in-law Roland Barkas has been so generous with his time, his chauffeuring, and his care that we have abandoned all hope of repaying him adequately.

With the same cheerful spirit of those friends, our readers/editors helped us select and improve our material with enthusiasm, or else they did a fine job of concealing the onerous nature of their crucial task. Thanks to Tom and Carol Aikenhead, Jim and Justine Hawley, Alison Roth, Jon Seed, and the many others on the committee.

We rely in this book more on photos than on words. We thank the SWCPA for some photos from their fine collection.

Finally, we are grateful to the authors of the guidebooks mentioned in this book and to the anonymous authors of the many pamphlets at local points of interest.

A view near Tintagel.

ABOUT THIS BOOK

From end to end for 630 miles England's South West Coast Path delights all travelers. Walkers on the Path stroll along beaches and climb to craggy heights. They visit ancient villages perched on the hills above protected harbors. They pass through meadows rolling to the edge of cliffs high above the surf. This book offers a view of one of the world's treasures.

Travelers come home with stories. After five years on the Path, two weeks each year, we have stories. In this book we include some of our adventures that we hope will be instructive.

We divide the book into two parts. The first part gives our impressions of the Path, as we traveled it day by day and year by year. In our daily trail descriptions we rate each day's walk for its scenic appeal. Our scenic ratings go from 0.0 (take a bus) to 5.0 (stunning).

In Part II we give advice and information for those who will walk all or part of the Path. We include a list of suggested guidebooks with a short description of each.

Our friend Liz Wallis, Administrator of the South West Coast Path Association, says she loves her job. "When I talk with people who call for information," she explains, "I know their experience on the Path will be far better than what they imagine."

We agree with Liz.

- Peter and Steve

ABOUT THE PATH ...
SMUGGLERS AND HIKERS

For centuries smugglers plied England's southern coast. On Lundy Island they turned their cannon against the Crown's customs agents and kept the island as their own.

Local people gave the Crown little support. In 1747 a gang of some thirty smugglers attacked the Customs House in Poole. As they rode off with their reclaimed contraband, the people of the villages en route cheered them on their way.

Rudyard Kipling in "A Smuggler's Song" describes the problem for the customs agents.

Five and twenty ponies
Trotting through the dark –
Brandy for the Parson,
'Baccy for the clerk;
Laces for a lady,
Letters for a spy,
And watch the wall, my darling,
While the gentlemen go by!

During the late eighteenth and early nineteenth centuries smuggling became more profitable than ever as government duties rose to pay for the continental wars. The government responded to increased smuggling with "Ye guard of ye coasts," or officially in 1822 the Coastguard Service.

The Coastguard had to be able to see every coastal cove in order to "inspect all creeks and bye-places," as their early mission stated. Patrolling on foot, the Coastguard created the Coast Path.

A typical hiking group pauses near Mawgan Porth.

Smuggling abated, and the Coastguard no longer needed its path, but people still used it as a link between seaside villages.

Thanks to the Ramblers Association, the National Trust, and above all the South West Coast Path Association, created in 1973, the Path now serves as the longest recreational trail in England. The central government supplies its major funding.

ABOUT THE AUTHORS

Steve Aikenhead and Peter Seed have a lot in common, starting with Linda, who is Steve's sister and Peter's wife. Linda always joins the two on their yearly walks, in spirit. She uses Steve's voice.

"Do you want these used Band-Aids that are on the floor?"

"You're putting the butter knife in the jam jar."

"If you dab the tip of the spout, it won't drip on the table."

In addition to Linda, the authors share an academic background: Yale. Steve passed through the ivied halls as quietly as a sleuth in a trench coat. Peter achieved greater visibility, joining a secret society.

Peter went on to Harvard Law School and was a partner in a law firm in Minnesota, his childhood home, where he raised his two children with Linda in charge. He lives now in Minnesota, Florida, Arizona, and New Zealand, unless he is traveling.

Steve in the time of his hair, 1971.

Steve is a teacher. As a child he lived in Connecticut. His second childhood unfolded in the San Francisco area in the 1960's. His third occurred in a small village north of the city. He now lives in a hilltop cabin he built in Vermont, unless he is trying to be helpful at the elementary school in California where he taught for many years.

Peter and Steve attended English schools in

the English Speaking Union's exchange program. Peter led the way at Harrow. Steve was at The Leys in Cambridge.

The English connection strengthened when Peter's daughter Nancy settled and married in England. On one of his visits with Nancy, Peter discovered the Coast Path. One small hike led to another, and now there is this book.

The authors have been hikers since youth. Steve at the age of 16 took a bus into the Smoky Mountains of North Carolina and managed to survive a week in the rain. Peter scaled the Grand Teton in Wyoming while in secondary school. That was the end of his rock climbing with ropes. Since then he has walked trails from Nepal to New Zealand.

Peter in Yellowstone National Part, 1971.

The authors travel in harmony. Peter tries to be neat, and Steve tries not to nag.

Steve had to train Peter in only one regard. Peter is solicitous. Steve hates sympathy. After Steve's every little slip, Peter would ask, "Are you all RIGHT?" Once trained, he would say, "I hope that hurt!"

Very little bothers these two. It doesn't matter to Steve that Peter's bicycle touring book sold more copies than all of Steve's publications combined. It doesn't matter to Peter that Steve causes countless delays by shopping. It doesn't even matter that Peter is a Republican and Steve is a Democrat.

What matters is that they love the outdoors, and they are buoyant.

CONTENTS

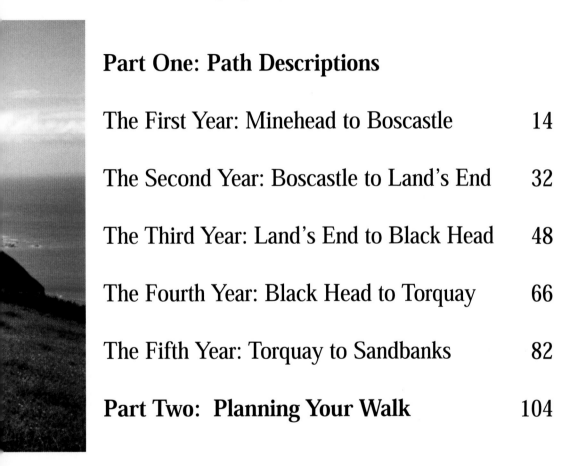

Part One: Path Descriptions

The

First

Year

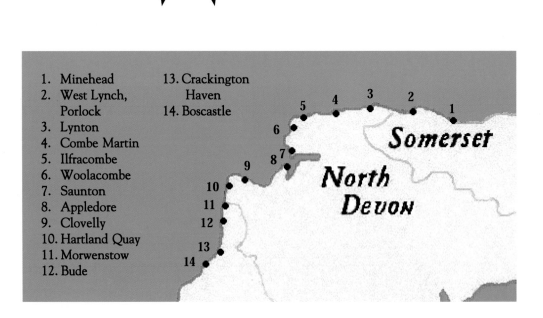

Somerset

North Devon

The First Day

Minehead to West Lynch: 7
miles, scenic rating 4.7
    The Coast Path begins at
Minehead, climbing to its
typical terrain: high, with
wonderful views. There are
options. The "very steep" trail is,
as promised, a hard climb. The
"rugged" trail is not too bad and
is prettier and closer to the coast
than the normal route. There are
wooded valleys, called combes,
and some steep climbs in this
opening stretch.
    West Lynch and its
neighbor Bossington are
sixteenth-century villages.

Above,
heading into
West Lynch.
Left, Peter
stands beside
foxgloves on
the "Rugged
Trail" above
Minehead.
Opposite, west
of Lynton.
Contents page,
south of
Crackington
Haven.

Right, Steve rests his injured shin after leaving Culbone. The wild Exmoor ponies, opposite, are near West Lynch. Peter pauses by foxgloves and sheep on the road to Lynmouth.

MY FOOT, THE HERO

During the second day of the great adventure an internal injury produces a red mark on my right shin. Whenever my foot strikes the top of a stile or a rock or root, I wince.

"Peter," I say that evening after shin inspection, "tomorrow I'm going to leave my pack here at the B & B and come back by bus at the end of the day to get it."

Since difficulty in walking downstairs is not a valid medical excuse, Peter the next day has to carry his pack. He swallows his Ibuprofen, and off we go. I leave him before mile two.

Three days later, when I am accustomed to my packless walking and bus routine, I watch Peter struggle up a muddy slope. He has orange mud on the bottom of his pants. He slips. He swears. He looks back at me.

"Why am I carrying a pack?!" he exclaims.

The next day he joins me on the bus.

Two days later we travel with Eva and Ro from Sweden. In an angst-laden tone, Eva asks, "Vy are ve carrying our packs?"

The next morning and each morning after that, our four packs travel in the back of a taxi to our next B & B.

- Steve

The Second Day

<u>West Lynch to Lynton</u>: 13 miles, scenic rating 4.8

At Culbone, not far from West Lynch, the smallest parish church in England is tucked into a wooded combe. On higher land beyond the church, farm gates frame sheep in pastures sloping to the sea. Farther on the traveler enters woods filled with massive rhododendron (best in late May), before climbing to spectacular cliff-side traverses and high farms. Lynton and its harbor at Lynmouth are in view from over a mile away.

THAT'S EASY FOR YOU TO SAY

Are you going to Woolacombe? Will you visit Ilfracombe? Combe Martin? You will sound clever if you pronounce the combe part as "coom." It's Celtic (that's "Keltic") for a wooded valley, so every time you see one on the map, you're in for a dip and a climb.

Are you going to walk on the quay? It's a wharf and is pronounced "key." Look for it in Hartland Quay and along any waterfront where boats load and unload.

Because place names in southwest England can be difficult to pronounce, our English in-law has helped us create some limericks as aids for proper pronunciation.

There was a young lady from Bude
Who liked to swim in the nude.
The men would admire her
And secretly desire her –
The rest I can't tell; it's too lewd.

There was a young lady from Clovelly
Who had a voluptuous belly.
She would wiggle her hips
And pout her red lips,
But sadly her feet were too smelly.

A maid who calls home Mevagissey
With me has been terribly prissy -
I wanted to flirt,
She wouldn't - it hurt,
But I'm sure that some day she will miss me.

Warning: this book contains limericks.

Left,
near the
Valley of
the
Rocks.
Below,
east of
Heddon's
Mouth.

The Third Day

<u>Lynton to Combe Martin</u>: 12 miles, scenic rating 5.0

A paved path above the sea turns to grass and heads inland to the Valley of the Rocks. The trail passes a tea house at the end of the valley, then hugs the side of a high cliff, giving dramatic views. Descending to Heddon Valley, the Path follows a stream to Hunters Inn. Strutting peacocks live there.

The route then climbs two massive open hills. The first of these, Great Hangman, is the high point of the South West Coast Path at 1,043 feet.

The Fourth Day

<u>Combe Martin to Woolacombe</u>:
13 miles, scenic rating 4.0

The first part of this section, to Ilfracombe around Widmouth Head, has some fine cliff-top views, but there is a caravan (RV) site at the prettiest harbor en route, and the Path follows a road into Hele, which is a fine place to live, but is not an attraction for walkers. The beautiful harbor of Ilfracombe is active with fishing boats. The rest of Ilfracombe is a large and bustling tourist center.

After escaping Ilfracombe, walkers enter a lovely section, passing through the village of Lee, nestled in its wooded river valley. The rest of the walk to Woolacombe is easy, along the coast.

Right, Ilfracombe Harbor, where the local fisherman, above, has put his fresh fish on ice. Opposite, above Lee Peter decides that this public path probably leads to the coast.

OFF PATH

About half a mile along the road that climbs out of Lee, as the coast begins to fade from view, something seems amiss.

I ask a farmer running a front-end bucket tractor how best to find the trail. With a friendly toothless grin, the farmer suggests that I stay the course and at the next T intersection, about a mile away, turn right to Mortehoe.

I nod and thank him, but half a mile later a public path seems to lead to the coast. I take that path. After crossing two fields, the trail vanishes at a farmhouse.

No one is in the house, but the chugging of a farm tractor from behind a barn gives me hope of help. Perhaps the driver can set me straight. Rounding the barn, I see the same farmer on the same tractor in the same place he had been before.

The farmer is greatly amused by my full circle. I assure him that this time I will take his advice to the letter.

When I get to the T intersection he mentioned, where he told me to turn right to Mortehoe, the sign shows Woolacombe to the left. Since Woolacombe is my destination, I turn left.

After a turn down a narrow lane that seems to lead to the coast, but quickly becomes a dead end, I flag down a trucker, who says I can get to Woolacombe a lot quicker if I go instead to Mortehoe. Defeated, I head for Mortehoe.

Not more than 500 feet on the road to Mortehoe, a large sign points to the Woolacombe Bay Trailer Park. Could this be a short cut to Woolacombe? A passing motorist tells me it is. I arrive in Woolacombe with plenty of time for tea.

Sometimes it's good to follow your instincts.

- Peter

The Fifth Day

<u>Woolacombe to Saunton</u>: 8.3 miles, scenic rating 4.2

Some of this stretch is along a beach road or on the beach itself. Some goes through high country. Around Baggy Point there are fine sea views and a view of the trail for miles ahead.

The best option after Baggy Point is along a hard-packed beach and then above a busy road through gorse that is home to a variety of birds.

The Sixth Day

<u>Saunton to Appledore</u>: 25 miles, scenic rating 3.0

    This was an easy section for us. We took the bus. As policy, we don't walk 25 miles through population centers.

    Anyone who walks this stretch will find it quite flat, with some estuaries, sand dunes, and walks on sea walls, old railway tracks, and roads.

    We give Appledore our highest rating. Explore the alleys, which the residents call streets.

In Appledore, above, in exchange for the trick removal of a thumb, the children regaled us with as many dirty jokes as we could desire.

Above, low tide at Instow. Opposite, a farmhouse at Baggy Point and the trail between Woolacombe and Saunton.

HEAVEN AND HELL

Today's walk from Westward Ho! to Clovelly, hereafter to be known as the Walk from Hell, falls apart after the first mile, when we zigzag up to a cliff top and plunge into the combe on the other side.

The trail is muddy and overgrown. My pack feels heavy. Warm humidity replaces sea breezes, and I slip in the mud and take a messy tumble more than once.

The thickest part of the trail is in National Trust property. The warden is out clearing the way. He complains that he has too much territory to cover and no volunteers to help.

We enter more woods with steep climbs. Though the tree cover provides shade, it eliminates the scenery and breezes that might have refreshed our souls. We endure five miles of sloppy, overgrown, enclosed, and hilly hiking before we descend into Buck's Mills, a small fishing village 400 years old.

Brought back to life by soup and milk shakes, we make our last climb out of the combe. We reach the cobblestones of the shaded Hobby Road, built by French prisoners during the Napoleonic wars. On a gentle slope we stride the three miles into Clovelly.

In Clovelly delivery carts rattle on the cobbles of 400 years ago. There are no cars. There are no tourist shops. A sled goes downhill loaded with milk and goods.

My daughter and her husband have come down from London. We have drinks in the sun on the edge of Clovelly's steep lane. Our laughter and talk mix with the sounds of the walkers and the carts on the lane.

- Peter

The Seventh Day

<u>Westward Ho! to Clovelly</u>: 12 miles, scenic rating 3.7

There are thickets, a lot of thick tree cover, and the usual ups and downs in this section, but the occasional sight of Clovelly in the distance, tumbling to the sea, makes the trip tolerable. The village of Buck's Mills has old homes that line a lane dropping to the sea. It also has a hotel worthy of a stop for lunch or more.

Clovelly is a picture-book village frozen in time that holds multitudes of visitors well. Cars must park above the village for a fee.

Below, Mr. E. Wilkinson, out for a walk, identifies the rare scarlet pimpernel. Clovelly's sixteenth-century seawall once protected 60 boats. Opposite, two of our family rest in Clovelly.

Below, a ship lies near Hartland Point, which the hikers, bottom, have just passed. Opposite, Peter contemplates the universe in the hut where the slightly mad Vicar of Morwenstow composed poems. The fields are between Hartland Quay and Morwenstow.

The Eighth Day

<u>Clovelly to Hartland Quay</u>: 10 miles, scenic rating 4.9

After a woodsy start, the Path rolls up and down through pastoral land with some marvelous cliff-top views. From Hartland Point the coast is rugged and craggy, its rock strata etched by the sea. The trail travels from cliff tops to rocky coves as it approaches the wildly dramatic Hartland Quay. Parts of this stretch are unsurpassed for beauty, though the journey is merely lovely and pleasant most of the way.

The Ninth Day

<u>Hartland Quay to Morwenstow</u>: 8 miles, scenic rating 5.0

On open terrain, the Path in this section is up, down, and spectacular. It eases into a high mellow walk through grassy slopes with occasional dips. Farm animals graze to the cliff's edge. Streams and a waterfall are en route.

Morwenstow's church and pub are worth a visit, as is Hawker's Hut, haunt of the eccentric Vicar of Morwenstow.

The Tenth Day

<u>Morwenstow to Bude</u>: 9 miles, scenic rating 4.8

      This stretch has extensive panoramas and dizzying views of sea-battered rocks at the base of its cliffs. The trail has some steep pitches until it reaches the sandstone cliffs overlooking the long beach at Bude, a mecca for hang gliders and surfers.

Above, a stile near Bude.
Right, International Adventures drops their young people over the edge in Bude.
Opposite, two young walkers climb from Crackington Haven.

The Eleventh Day

<u>Bude to Crackington Haven</u>: 9 miles, scenic rating 4.8

    After the Path leaves the populous area around Bude, it becomes its dippy self with great views of the sea and of verdant fields and valleys. On a clear day the high tors of Dartmoor are on the horizon.

    The Haven is a rocky refuge for a few homes and one hotel.

ACHIEVEMENT

    About every day we tell a local where we've been hiking, and the local says, "That's a good walk, but I think you'll find tomorrow's stretch a good deal more difficult."

    The next day we feel pretty good after walking that more difficult bit without too much trouble, and that day's local says, "Oh, yes, but your really nasty section comes up tomorrow."

    And that day's local says, "Well, you're in for it tomorrow."

    So we rush to our trail guide, which tells us we are foolish even to attempt the next day's route. We will mount to giddy heights, tumble into deep valleys, rise strenuously, dip to sea level, only to rise again … . The word "severe" appears in the trail description.

    But another tomorrow comes and goes with no problems, and we feel proud of our hiking prowess.

    On our last day, a comment made by an oncoming walker lessens our sense of accomplishment.

    Philip points to his brother and says, "That's Matthew. He's two." Philip is three.

The Twelfth Day

<u>Crackington Haven to Boscastle</u>: 7 miles, scenic rating 5.0

High cliffs with sheer rock faces drop to a green surf. Seagulls swirl and cry. There is some strenuous walking, and some easy, all with views both inland and seaward.

Lower Boscastle is Cornwall's answer to Devon's Clovelly. It is well preserved and rightfully crowded. Upper Boscastle, one long street, is even older than lower Boscastle and is worth a visit.

Above, north of Boscastle.
Left, north of Boscastle.
Opposite, above: the oldest building in lower Boscastle is this fourteenth-century cottage, now a shop.
Opposite, below, in Upper Boscastle: "Pardon me. Isn't it lunch time?"

The Second Year

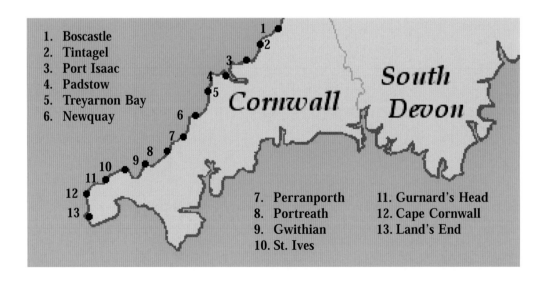

1. Boscastle
2. Tintagel
3. Port Isaac
4. Padstow
5. Treyarnon Bay
6. Newquay

Cornwall

South Devon

7. Perranporth
8. Portreath
9. Gwithian
10. St. Ives

11. Gurnard's Head
12. Cape Cornwall
13. Land's End

The First Day

Boscastle to Tintagel: 4 miles, scenic rating 5.0

    The Path cuts around the headland above the narrow harbor of Boscastle and then on one side overlooks green fields framed by stonewalls and on the other side the sea. The trail drops to Rocky Valley, where a wooded stream leads to Trevillet Mill House, a good spot for lunch or tea.

    Advertising signs blemish the village of Tintagel but leave untouched the remains of a twelfth-century castle high on a rocky promontory. Some think King Arthur's castle was here.

Above, near Rocky Valley. Left, the Old Post Office in Tintagel is fourteenth century. Opposite, a drop to the sea from Climbing Rocks after Bosigran Cliffs.

HOLD THAT MUSE

We are in a dangerous situation. We have started composing poems.

The danger is that we might recite our poems to someone else. Tossing off an occasional phrase out loud is like saying, "I think I'll have just one potato chip."

The next thing you know, people will be staring at us blankly after being drenched by a rain of cliché and misused metaphor.

High on a molded cliff we see
White steeds gallop on a turquoise plain.
Seagulls mark mid-air
Between dark walls of stone.
Gentle air embraces us
Where we pause on the edge of time.

It's so beautiful! We mean the landscape.

The Second Day

<u>Tintagel to Port Isaac</u>: 8 miles,
scenic rating 5.0

Steps drop into deep
valleys and climb steeply up,
making legs burn. In many
places abandoned slate quarries
and their ruined structures match
the loneliness of the sea crashing
on the rocks below.

Port Isaac is a town of
old cottages and inns, narrow
crooked streets, and a tiny
harbor with the few fishing boats
it can hold. You must walk
single-file through Squeeze-ee-
belly Alley.

Above, a
tough climb
on the
approach to
Port Isaac
can lead to
terrace
refreshments,
left, on the
edge of
town.
Opposite, a
view not far
beyond
Tintagel.

The Third Day

<u>Port Isaac to Padstow</u>: 11.7 miles, scenic rating 5.0

A high path overlooking the rocky coast winds for three miles past large farms inland. Doyden Castle, which is a folly, and Doyden House sit bleakly on exposed sites. Craggy promontories – The Rumps, The Mouls, Pentire Point – once held Iron Age forts. On this route there are remains from the mining of past ages.

The trail slopes to St. Enodoc Church, deep in the dunes, and then reaches the ferry to Padstow, home of Elizabethan Prideaux Place.

Left, the sand has been blowing on St. Enodoc Church since the fifteenth century.
Below, sea gazers at Pentire Point, just west of The Rumps.
Opposite, a sea tunnel east of The Rumps.

IRON AGE FORTS

Not far from Doyden Castle, Steve is pulled by the allure of an Iron Age fort on a promontory known as The Rumps.

As we approach The Rumps, I see at a distance what looks like high jagged boulders at the tip of the headland. Are those jagged boulders the fort? We race on, and when we get closer, we see... rocks.

We have rushed through the Iron Age fortifications. They turn out to be two parallel mounds cut by the trail about 500 feet behind us.

Every time I see an archaeological find like this, I feel like an insensitive Philistine. When I return to the low earthen bulges, I cannot detect any difference between them and similar rises caused solely by nature. But excavations have confirmed that the mounds were once faced with stone and were part of the defenses of England's warring Iron Age ancestors.

- Peter

Above, top: near Trevone. The lighthouse is at Trevose Head.

The Fourth Day

<u>Padstow to Treyarnon Bay</u>: 11 miles, scenic rating 4.2 includes 5.0

The early stretch of this walk has views to worry acrophobes. Inland, sheep dot a patchwork of lush hillsides divided by stone walls.

The latter part of the walk includes a sewage plant, caravan park (RVs), and some difficult beach walking.

Surfers enjoy Harlyn Bay.

The Fifth Day

<u>Treyarnon Bay to Newquay</u>: 13 miles, scenic rating 4.6

The long view suggests that a straight, level walk lies ahead, but the cliffs are dissected by finger-like coves, and the unstable land in many places slips to the sea. It is wise to heed the warnings to "Stay Away From the Edge." There are many steep steps to climb before the route slopes to long beaches.

Newquay is a large and clean town, with flowers and parks. Its bustling shops and lanes along the cliff front teem with tourists.

Above, a gate frames a garden near Porthcothan Beach. The park below is in Newquay.

Below, catching the air at Perran Beach and a view of the sea near Holywell Bay. Opposite, cloned cows south of St. Agnes and the rocky coastline between St. Agnes and Portreath.

The Sixth Day

<u>Newquay to Perranporth</u>: 12 miles, scenic rating 4.2

After crossing the Gannel River, by boat or on a footway, depending on the tide, the hiker climbs to high views and dips to coves and beaches. There is a dim 600-year old pub at Holywell. Perran Beach stretches three miles to Perranporth, which at low tide overlooks vast glistening sands spreading from its river mouth. Hang gliders sail from the cliffs at Perran Beach.

The Seventh Day

<u>Perranporth to Portreath</u>: 12 miles, scenic rating 4.3

The trail rises high above the sands of Perranporth to give a tour of tin mining shafts and skeletal structures. Landing strips for World War II fighter planes hide behind bunkers on a cliff near Perranporth.

The Trevaunce Point Hotel, early 1700's, offers a high garden spot for refreshment. After the hotel there are some spectacular views, then more tin mines and military sites before the trail descends to the small town of Portreath.

NO BAD DAYS

Unless you get blown off a cliff, there are no bad days on the Coast Path.

While I'm jogging the Path near St. Ives, I hit some nettle that eats its way through my shirt, I klonk my elbow when I slip on a stone, and after returning my windblown hat from a flowering bush to my head, I discover that a bee has crawled inside my hat.

None of the above matters. The Path is lovely, and the church at Lelant with the Celtic crosses is worth a little discomfort.

I also have the enjoyment of seeing whether a runner's bee-stung brain will swell up and explode, or whether the bee poison will seep into his spinal cord and paralyze him. Since all I feel is the equivalent of a glob of nettle juice on top of my head, I rate the run a success.

It does not matter that when I return to St. Ives for medication, I get hopelessly lost. Getting lost in the winding streets of St. Ives is the best way to see the place.

It does not matter that the warm vegie pasty I bought for lunch moistens its way through the bag and falls PLOP SPLAT on the cobblestones. The locals assure me that seagulls, called flying rats here, will get the bit I leave behind. The rest is good.

Bad is what happened to the people who attacked the Iron Age defenses up at The Rumps.

Bad was the fate of the hundreds of ships wrecked at Doom Bar near Stepper Point.

Bad was the loss of 31 tin miners at Levant when the block broke loose.

But your fate walking on the Coast Path will be happy as long as you start crawling in a high wind.

- Steve

The Eighth Day

<u>Portreath to Gwithian, St. Ives</u>:
18 miles, scenic rating 5.0 to
Gwithian

    Sheer cliffs, jagged reefs,
and a churning sea tempt the
photographer at every turn.
Eventually the heights taper to a
long beach and to the narrow
village of Gwithian.

    If not purists, walkers
might want to skip the flat
populated area from Gwithian to
St. Ives, to enjoy more time in
the crooked streets of St. Ives.

Above, a typical scene in St. Ives.
Below, approaching Godrevy Point and
Godrevy Island, inspiration for Virginia
Woolf's novel, *To the Lighthouse*.

Below, east of Zennor Head. Opposite, top: Zennor, a short distance from the Path. The bovine lookout guards the route to Gurnard's Head.

The Ninth Day

St. Ives to Gurnard's Head: 8 miles, scenic rating 4.8

Some boggy rough spots don't spoil a varied walk. At first the trail traverses slopes of thick, scrubby grass and scattered outcrops. Later a roller coaster section gives views of headlands reaching into the sea. On the inland side, small fields separated by stone walls are preserved as they were in the Bronze Age 4,000 years ago.

LOST

Hello. I'm lost. Could you tell me the way
To Pepper Hole, Butter Hole, or Booby Bay?
They're close to the place I'm supposed to have been
By three. Penallick? Penhallic? It begins with a Pen.
Near Diggory Island? I think it's just north
Of Porth Mear, Porthcothan, or Mawgan Porth.
I know at Porth-cadiack, Porthgwidden, Hell's Mouth,
Towanroath, or Porthtowan I'd be too far south.
Not Pentire or Pengirt, but well past the Zawn,
It sounds like some place to which I have gone
Back at Dizzard and Pigsback, Squench Rocks, and the Strangles.
Pencannow? Oh, dear – it's jingles and jangles.
Wait! Silly me. It's not Pen. Just listen
To this – it's Porth! Porthmissen!

- Steve

Right, Steve is off Path, scrambling to the top of Gurnard's Head.
Below, the horses graze near Cape Cornwall. The cove is near Pendeen Watch.

The Tenth Day

<u>Gurnard's Head to Cape Cornwall</u>: 7 miles, scenic rating 4.8

Those who like rocky precipitous heights might scale the spine of Gurnard's Head. Beyond that promontory, the trail cuts through an uncultivated region with open views. There is a lighthouse at Pendeen Watch.

Extensive tin mining sites with half-ruined stone buildings give the next stretch a war-zone appearance. At the end of the day the cropped fields of Cape Cornwall receive the traveler.

The Eleventh Day

<u>Cape Cornwall to Land's End</u>: 6 miles, scenic rating 4.7

As the miles pass by, Land's End comes more clearly into view. There are descents to the sea and to the popular surfing beach at Sennen Cove, but most of the route is up top on gentle terrain. Horses are in the fields, and walkers appear more frequently as the trail approaches England's western tip, which is crowded with tourists.

Above, Land's End, about a mile past the beach at Sennen Cove, below.

The

Third

Year

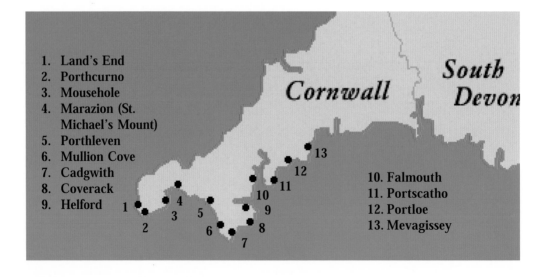

1. Land's End
2. Porthcurno
3. Mousehole
4. Marazion (St. Michael's Mount)
5. Porthleven
6. Mullion Cove
7. Cadgwith
8. Coverack
9. Helford

10. Falmouth
11. Portscatho
12. Portloe
13. Mevagissey

Cornwall

South Devon

The First Day

Land's End to Porthcurno: 5.5 miles, scenic rating 5.0

Many hikers think that this is one of the best pieces of Path from Minehead to Poole. High cliffs and sculpted rocks rising from the sea keep photographers busy. Soft grassy paths lead to rocky headlands.

The haven of Porthgwarra offers refreshment. Porthcurno offers much more by being the home of the Minack Theatre, carved into a rock precipice that plunges to the sea.

Left, Peter looks east from near Land's End.
The perch above is east of Gwennap Head. Opposite, a cat relaxes in Perranuthnoe.

FOOLISH WOMAN

Since childhood, Rowena Cade loved homemade theater productions. When she was 38, she and her friends needed a stage for "The Tempest." Rowena looked at the craggy headland near her home and thought, "This is the place."

Someone must have said, "My dear, don't be foolish. You can't build anything on a precipice like that."

That year of 1931-32 Rowena apprenticed herself to her gardeners Billy Rawlings and Tom Angove. Sewing was her job experience. She looked frail.

The three workers cut granite by hand and inched the stones into place. They shoveled earth and small stones down the slope to their site. One wheelbarrow plunged over the edge.

That summer "The Tempest" was lit by battery-powered lights, car lights, and a moon whose beams glittered across the bay far below. Over the next seven years Rowena and the two men made improvements.

After the Second World War the army destroyed the theater while clearing coastal defenses.

"You are over 50," someone must have said. "Be happy with wonderful memories."

Rowena rebuilt the theater. She, Billy, and Tom added an access road, a car park, and a flight of 90 steps from the beach. They turned a gun post into the box office. When Billy died, Rowena at the age of 73 became the master builder.

When she could not afford granite, she developed her own artistic techniques for working with cement. On her back she brought bags of sand from the beach. Single-handed, she brought up twelve 15-foot beams, salvage from a wreck.

"My dear, you are almost 80," someone must have said. "You must stop."

Rowena worked through all weather and through every winter until she was in her mid-eighties.

When she died, the Minack Theatre lived on.

The Second Day

<u>Porthcurno to Mousehole</u>: 8 miles, scenic rating 4.7

     Our rating is higher with a stop for tea at Cove Cottage near St. Loy. It's near tops if the trail is clear. This stretch is a high walk with dips to picturesque beaches and villages. There are short detours to craggy knobs and headlands, and to the barely balanced Logan Rock.

     Mousehole (Mowzel) is a town of old stone homes, narrow streets, and a protected harbor.

Rowena Cade created the Minack Theatre, above, at Porthcurno.
At Penberth Cove, below, Phoenicians once traded for Cornish tin.

Above, top: the St. Aubyn family has lived in the castle on St. Michael's Mount since 1660.
Above, the promenade is one of many places to visit in Penzance.
Opposite, top: Steve on a stile near Prussia Cove.
Opposite, bottom: Peter, between Trewavas Head and Porthleven.

The Third Day

Mousehole to Marazion: 7 miles, scenic rating 3.6

The walk up from Mousehole through the village of Paul and down across the fields overlooking Newlyn and Penzance is pleasant, assuming the walker catches the turn out of Paul. Penzance is large and busy with a wide seaside promenade. From Penzance the Path follows the beach for three miles to Marazion.

There the grand castle of St. Michael's Mount, open to the public, rises on top of an island pinnacle.

The Fourth Day

<u>Marazion to Porthleven</u>: 10.5 miles, scenic rating 4.9

Until Trevean Cove the path is merely pleasant walking, but after that point there are gorgeous sea scenes, dramatic plunges, and pastoral landscapes that gain our highest rating.

Prussia Cove is a cluster of stone homes and a former haven for smugglers. The fishing town of Porthleven has character and charm. The long beach at Praa Sands is a popular holiday spot.

Below, the view from the top of Halzephron Cliff.
Opposite, top: beautiful cows live at Penrose Estate.
Opposite, bottom: nettle, near Lamorna.

The Fifth Day

<u>Porthleven to Mullion Cove</u>: 7 miles plus a 4 mile side trip, scenic rating 5.0

The fields and waters of bucolic Penrose Estate reward the effort of a detour from Loe Bar. Back on the Path, which generally runs wide and smooth on this stretch, there are spectacular views of the rugged coastline and of The Lizard, England's southernmost point.

The fishing village of Mullion Cove follows its one street uphill. At the top of the climb, a mile up, the old homes of Mullion lie close to their ancient church.

NETTLE WAY

Kevin from Exeter meets me on the Path near Lamorna. We move on together, and in the course of our conversation he says, "I've walked all over the world."

"Is there a lovelier path anywhere?" I ask him, using proper English phrasing.

He smiles. "I don't think so," he admits.

I nod, but in my mind I hesitate. Today we have been walking Nettle Way. Red bumps cover my throbbing legs.

"It's a wonderful path," I continue, "worth a little nettle."

"If you've been stung," he says, "there is an antidote called dock leaf."

"If?" I ask. "I love British understated humor."

"We are masters of that," he concedes.

He starts to search for the medicinal plant. "It grows wherever there is nettle," he explains.

I am thinking we are about to see the exception to that rule when Kevin points and says, "There's some!"

It's a large, shiny oval leaf, unlike the bristly-looking nettle, whose oils it must conquer.

"Just rub it on," Kevin says.

He demonstrates, and I try it.

"It works!" I exclaim.

Kevin smiles. I thank him.
He is correct on dock leaf and
correct on the beauty of the Path.

- Steve

Above, fishermen rest in Cadgwith. The thatched house below is at Church Cove, an inlet next to Landewednack.

The Sixth Day

<u>Mullion Cove to Cadgwith</u>: 11 miles, scenic rating 5.0

Cliff face and shipwreck rocks predominate past Lizard Point. Flowers and rolling farmlands lure the photographer.

Kynance Cove is strewn with small rocky islands. Landewednack is a one-lane village sliding to the sea. Cadgwith's parabolic lane drops and rises steeply to and from a small active harbor.

The Seventh Day

<u>Cadgwith to Coverack</u>: 7 miles, scenic rating 4.8

The route to Kennack Sands is high and lovely, with dips to beaches and coves. After Kennack Sands, Pedn Boar (Black Head) is striking, and until shortly before Coverack the Path keeps a top rating. Coverack is a large attractive village curving around its harbor.

Above, the seawall in Coverack.
Left, an Exmoor pony, imported to keep the gorse down, walks the Path near Pedn Boar.

YOU TAKE THE HIGH ROAD

After we traverse the hillside this morning past the last row of houses at Coverack's east end, Steve disappears into the mist, and I trudge along, scanning for the Coast Path's acorn marker that assures me I am on track.

I come to a huge working quarry where a barely discernable trail heads to the left. I choose a path that goes straight ahead under a conveyor belt, but moments later my path becomes a road that dumps me onto a beach flanked by a sheer rock wall.

After circling the beach twice, I spy an acorn marker. I follow that trail leading inland. A mile from the coast, having seen no more acorn markers, I wander into a village called St. Keverne. There I give up on the Coast Path and follow the roads overland to Helford.

The back roads turn out to be pleasant, certain, free of mist, and over five miles shorter than the Coast Path. After a shandy and sandwich, I walk into Helford in less than an hour in good spirits. I locate a comfortable spot on the Coast Path, read a newspaper, and wait.

Steve eventually comes up the path, but does not see me. I call out and ask him if he is lost. Stunned, he says he thought I was miles behind. I learn that at the juncture before the conveyor belt he took the barely discernable trail and managed to connect with the Coast Path.

A long route or a short route can get you to the same place.

- Peter

Right, Frenchman's Creek, near Helford. A secluded trail follows the edge of the river.
Opposite, Helford.

The Eighth Day

<u>Coverack to Helford</u>: 13 miles, scenic rating 4.8

The first part of this route, to Lowland Point, is through pasture along the shore. The walker then has a choice: officially through quarry or up the hill on a public footpath to St. Keverne and on through rural landscape to another pleasant village, Porthallow. Back on the Path, fields slope to an increasingly rocky shore.

On Gillan Creek the small village of St. Anthony has a fine church. Boating activity there includes rentals. Nearby Helford on its quiet inlet is golden at sunset and marvelous at any time of day. Frenchman's Creek, the setting for Daphne DuMaurier's romantic novel by that title, is a short walk from Helford.

Top, the Path drops to the sea close to Falmouth.
Bottom, the beach at Maen Porth.
Opposite, a feline walker rests near Portscatho.
Place House is across from Falmouth.

The Ninth Day

<u>Helford to Falmouth</u>: 10 miles, scenic rating 4.9
Until the small beach of Maen Porth, this section is superb. Lush fields roll to the sea and to wide rivers busy with boats. After Maen Porth the trail rises high above the sea, but there are no more soft green pastures. Helford Passage, Durgan, and the Church at St. Mawgan with its garden on the seaward side all win top ratings. The original name of the large port city of Falmouth was Moneycomequick.

The Tenth Day

<u>Falmouth to Portscatho</u>: 7.5 miles, scenic rating 4.8

To St. Anthony Head the Path is as lovely as it can be. The ferryboat rides, the Fal River, St. Mawes, and the Manor House in Place are all wonderful. The Path traverses tabletop farmland and leads the hiker beneath some grand trees.

After St. Anthony Head the walk is fairly easy, sometimes past cultivated land and sometimes through gorse, above the sea and rocky coast. The views are open, but not dramatic.

Below, approaching Nare Head.
Opposite: Portloe, where pounding surf in the narrow cove prevented the lifeguards from ever launching their boats in 17 years of desired service.

The Eleventh Day

<u>Portscatho to Portloe</u>: 7 miles, scenic rating 4.95

There are lots of high pastures in this section and lots of sea views. The Path dips to scenic beaches and has a notable climb to Nare Head, whose rocky height rises above the thick growth below. Broom Parc Trust House is en route.

Portloe is a charming village served by a single lane. Its tiny harbor is treacherous in storms. In summer red poppies dot the trailside above the town.

POINTS

"All right, Peter, pronounce the name of this village."

"Um. Cudworth? Cadwich?"

"Ha."

"All right, smarty, which B & B did we stay in last night?"

"Um."

"Ha."

The correct choice of divergent paths, accompanied by the incorrect choice by the companion, who shows up last when the trails meet, merits a victory dance by the winner, arms flung skyward in a V. On those competing routes the winner is disqualified if he breaks into a run en route or emerges bloodied by thorns or stung by nettle.

Points are given for finding an ideal photo site. They are lost for falling off a cliff.

Today Peter and I walk together, off Path, I in the lead. I come to the Coast Path on the other side of a barbed wire fence. This discovery justifies a small gloat of satisfaction. I have found the Path.

A sign warns, "Danger. Wire electrified."

I announce the danger. Then I drop to my stomach and crawl under the wire at the point of maximum clearance. I am halfway through, my face close to the moist earth, when Peter speaks from my right.

"Are you sure that's the best way?" he asks.

He is two yards away, standing on top of a stile that gives safe passage over the fence.

Minus 100 points.

- Steve

The Twelfth Day

<u>Portloe to Mevagissey</u>: 12 miles, scenic rating 5.0

To Dodman Point, steep slopes drop to the sea. The Path runs through pastures and through gorse, past coves and stony dwellings. After Dodman, sheep and cattle abound.

Green fields give entrance to the harbor town of Mevagissey, which is a bit touristy, but is at heart a village of narrow streets and old inns.

MURDER AND ESCAPE

On the wide grassy path leading into Mevagissey, we meet an elderly gentleman walking his dog.

He points to a nearby low cliff and tells of Sir Henry Bodrugan, a loser in the War of the Roses. When men loyal to King Henry VII pursued Sir Henry, the nobleman on his galloping steed leaped off the cliff and into the surf to escape to France on a waiting ship.

Our companion also shows us a house on the water and tells of the German resident who during the Second World War was rumored to be a spy. He used to look out to sea through his telescope. Three days after the rumors began, his body was found at the foot of the cliffs.

The last story he tells is of a man who lived in one of the heavily shuttered homes facing the sea at Portmellon, outside of Mevagissey. During storms waves break over these two-story buildings.

In the night on such an occasion, when the power was out, the man awoke and headed downstairs. A wave crashed open the front door, surged up the stairs, and pulled him into deep water, where he was swirled and slammed about, drowning. Then the force of the sea broke down the back door, and the man was poured out of his house, caught up in the water rushing through. His injuries were minor.

Left, the homes at Portmellon have shutters of double strength because the storm surge sometimes goes over the wall.
Opposite, top: near Dodman Point above Bow Beach.
Opposite, bottom: Dodman Point.

The

Fourth

Year

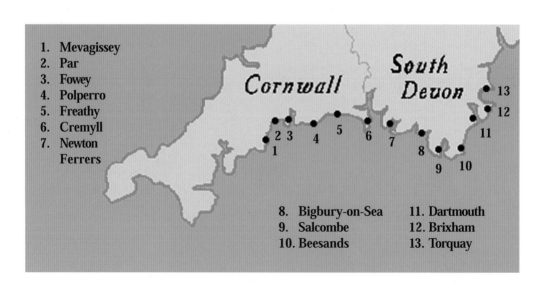

1. Mevagissey
2. Par
3. Fowey
4. Polperro
5. Freathy
6. Cremyll
7. Newton
    Ferrers

8. Bigbury-on-Sea
9. Salcombe
10. Beesands

11. Dartmouth
12. Brixham
13. Torquay

The First Day

Mevagissey to Par: 11.5 miles, scenic rating 3.8

Before Pentewan the most notable feature of this walk is a caravan (RV) park.

The middle stretch, from Pentewan to Charlestown, is high and lovely. The trail often borders or traverses fields filled with sheep or cows. The bulk of Black Head promontory looms in the distance.

After Charlestown hikers stroll past a golf course and through a clay works plant.

Above, Penare Point, on the way to Black Head. Left, not far past Black Head. Opposite, a seagull rests near Looe.

Top, Steve will find Fowey around the corner.

Bottom, three gigs race on the Fowey River. Each gig carries no more than six oarsmen, a historic limit set by the Coastguard, who feared being outrun by smugglers.

The Second Day

Par to Fowey: 6 miles, scenic rating 4.8

Once past Par, the Path is high above the sea on the way to the green fields of Gribbin Head. From there to Fowey the serenity of the Path earns it our highest rating.

Fowey is an old town whose pastel and whitewashed buildings line the hillside in tiers above the wide Fowey River. The Hall Walk, which leaves from Fowey, is a wooded circle trail with many fine views.

The Third Day

Fowey to Polperro: 7.1 miles, scenic rating 4.9

Our guidebook describes this section as "probably the toughest stretch of walking on the South Cornwall coast," but the pain of ascending the steep grassy hills is rewarded by views of towering cliffs and of sandy coves at the mouths of the valleys.

After Pencarrow Head grazing land yields to gorse, with views of distant promontories. Polperro's nook is beside a small harbor protected by rock and jetty.

Above, the streets of Polperro are too narrow for cars to enter. Below, on top of Raphael Cliff, west of Polperro.

TWO WAYS TO GO

I walk the promenade at Portwrinkle to a beach at the other end. Except for a friendly vendor who occupies a cabana, only one family has stayed this late, and they are packing up.

The vendor, whose name is Tony, tells me that he let Steve use his cell phone to call the owner of tonight's B & B. It's located about two miles away in the countryside. The proprietress, Kathy, offered to pick Steve up, but after receiving directions, he decided to walk the rest of the way.

I'm beat, so I buy a pop and agonize aloud about whether I should call for a car ride. Tony settles the issue by offering to take me to the B & B in his car as soon as he finishes closing up shop.

On the coastal road Tony and I spot Steve's bobbing head on the seaward side of a hedgerow that separates him from the road. He is going full tilt and disappears over a rise. We decide that, rather than try to find him, I should greet him at the door when he arrives at the B & B.

An hour later Kathy gets a call from Steve. He overshot by three miles the road he should have taken to the B & B.

- Peter

The Fourth Day

<u>Polperro to Freathy</u>: 16 miles, scenic rating 4.7

Polperro to Looe is neither dramatic nor pastoral, but has high sea views. Looe to Portwrinkle has breathtaking cliff-edge views, busy beaches, and shaded woods. Beyond that village, walkers have on one side the sea rising to the sky and on the other side fields stretching to the moors miles away.

East Looe is a crazy quilt of shops and houses facing West Looe across a harbor spanned by an arched stone bridge.

Above, Steve looks for Looe, whose harbor stream, below, is at low tide. Opposite, a field west of Looe.

TWO ENCOUNTERS

At an overlook on high ground I meet an elderly woman sitting on a bench. She is reading her book, with a baby carriage by her side. I look down, prepared to make the appropriate cooing sounds. Looking back at me is a dog, wrapped in a blanket.

"Emma," the lady explains, barely looking up from her book, "is just too frail to climb the hill."

Later I amble down a gentle hill, taking in the scenery. A young lady with two puppies on a leash charges up the hill on the same path. I do a jig to avoid squashing the yelping critters, but stumble and nearly fall.

"Felled by two puppies!" the lady calls out as she whips by me with her brood.

- Peter

The Fifth Day

<u>Freathy to Cremyll</u>: 9 miles, scenic rating 4.8

After leaving the road and the hillside bungalows at Freathy, the Path heads out generally in the open towards Rame Head. This great knob topped by a stone chapel 600 years old gives striking views. The Path remains lovely into Cawsand/Kingsand, old villages of narrow streets above Cawsand Bay. The final leg into Cremyll is pleasant walking. Near Cremyll the estate at Edgcumbe has broad lawns that slope to the sea.

Left, the Path heads up to Rame Head chapel. Rame is Cornish for ram's head. King Ethelred's uncle gave Rame to Tavistock Abbey in 981. The current chapel was licensed for mass in 1397.
Above, from Rame Head looking west. Opposite, from Rame Head chapel, looking northeast.

The Sixth Day

<u>Cremyll to Newton Ferrers</u>: 11 miles, scenic rating 4.2 includes 5.0

From Cremyll we took the ferry and bus to the Barbican in Plymouth, and then the ferry to Mountbatten Point. Our mileage begins there. Plymouth has points of interest for the hiker who walks through.

Once away from the city of Plymouth, the Path offers frequent views of Plymouth Sound and looks back at Plymouth from the headland. There is nothing that compels photography before Wembury Beach. After that the walk to Newton Ferrers is a jewel of undulating fields and boat-dotted rivers.

The whitewashed buildings of Newton Ferrers and Noss Mayo face each other across a tributary to the River Yealm.

The Seventh Day

<u>Newton Ferrers to Bigbury-on-Sea</u>: 14 miles, scenic rating 5.0

There is one drop to a caravan park, and some shaded woods, but otherwise this section is high, wide, and open. The first four miles are on Lord Revelstoke's grassy carriageway. Rolling pasture is inland. Hikers cross the River Erme on foot at low tide.

Bigbury-on-Sea has a spacious sea view. A "sea tractor" runs to and from Burgh Island when the causeway is under water. At low tide visitors walk to the island.

Above, the ruined church of St. Peter the Poor Fisherman in a caravan park at Stoke Beach. Left, hikers on Lord Revelstoke's carriageway. In the 1880's Lord Revelstoke hired local unemployed to build this track. When they needed more work, he increased the width from 7 to 10 feet. Opposite, Steve enters Newton Ferrers.

Above, Bigbury-on-Sea in the background and Moss in the foreground, as Peter and his son-in-law John set off for Hope. Right, the birds on the ridgeline at Inner Hope are the signature of the thatcher.
Opposite, between Hope and Salcombe.

The Eighth Day

<u>Bigbury-on-Sea to Salcombe</u>: 13.7 miles, scenic rating 5.0

The route to Hope above sandy beaches and over verdant hills is not difficult and includes spectacular views.

The section from Hope to Salcombe is rightly acclaimed as one of the most scenic of the entire Coast Path. The walker enjoys dramatic drops to the sea, lofty views, and inland fields. The giant promontory of Bolt Tail looms just beyond Hope.

The village of Outer Hope overlooks a cove. The long village of Salcombe hugs a hill above a boat-filled harbor.

HOPE

Hope is actually two villages, Outer Hope and Inner Hope. Both hug the coastline and are joined by a single road. They share a sandy cove. We first pass Outer Hope that holds the high ground and has all the trappings of a small modern resort town.

Inner Hope is at the bottom of the hill a hundred yards on and is a smaller and much older village than Outer Hope. A thatched general store, a whitewashed pub, and a cluster of fishermen's cottages surround the village square.

One commentator dubbed the villages Hope Present and Hope Past.

The Ninth Day

<u>Salcombe to Beesands</u>: 12 miles, scenic rating 4.8

The Path is high and stunning from Salcombe to Prawle Point, which is the final rocky promontory of this section. For miles the steep-sided trail snakes past weathered outcrops. Gara Rock Hotel, overlooking a plunge to the sea, offers refreshments. Gammon Head is a spur with a spine of schist.

The remainder of the walk features some pleasant walking by the sea and a pastoral descent to Beesands, a quiet one-lane village facing the beach.

Above, Lannacombe Beach below Start Point.
Right, Peter after descending from Prawle Point has met a gentleman who will staff the point's Coastguard hut, tracking ships and helping hikers. There are so many volunteers for the post that none serve more than 4 hours a week.

Left, the village of Torcross has Slapton Sands on the Channel side and freshwater Slapton Ley on the other.

Below, Dartmouth Castle. Henry VIII built this castle and Kingswear Castle on the other side of the river Dart. Defenders of the town could raise a chain between the two castles to deter invaders.

The Tenth Day

<u>Beesands to Dartmouth</u>: 5 miles, scenic rating 4.2

From the tidy village of Torcross, whose homes follow a long arc of beach, the Path stays low by lake and sea. Busy roads ensue, but the bus ride from Strete Gate or Strete to the far side of Stoke Fleming saves the hiker 5 miles of heavy traffic. The stretch from Stoke Fleming to Dartmouth is at first a paved path, though the drivers of occasional cars seem to think it's a road. Then comes some lovely walking on precipitous slopes above the sea.

Two stolid castles guard Dartmouth's harbor.

The Eleventh Day

<u>Dartmouth to Brixham</u>: 10.8 miles, scenic rating 4.8

After Kingswear, across from Dartmouth, the Path rises to views of turquoise coves and grand Scots pines, the giant bonsai of these hills. There are leafy tunnels through the woods and strenuous climbs opening to wide expanses of sea and fields. To Sharkham Point the Path receives our highest rating. The rest, though of less appeal, includes two Napoleonic forts.

The inner harbor at Brixham is busy with shoppers and proprietary seagulls.

The Twelfth Day

<u>Brixham to Torquay</u>: 8.4 miles, not rated

After a stroll through dark woods, travelers have a chance to see how the English care for one of their population centers. We don't know how to rate this section, but the Goodrington-Paignton-Torquay area, though not as lovely as a historic village, is tidy and a good place to live.

The towns have a variety of attractions. Cockington, outside of Torquay, is a finely preserved village of medieval times, with a large park that slopes from the main estate. Cockington draws many visitors.

Above, the dark woods are east of Brixham. Right, Cockington Court. Opposite, top: Scots pines, below Coleton Fishacre. Opposite, bottom: the couple approaching are walking not far east of Coleton Fishacre Gardens, east of Dartmouth. The photographer is behind a fence.

The

Fifth

Year

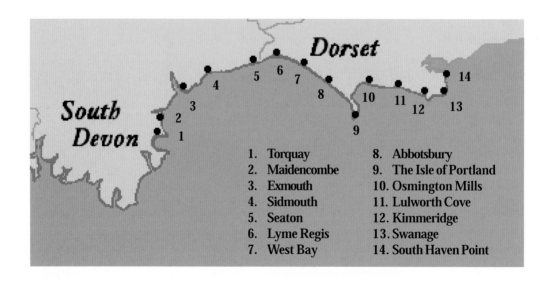

Dorset

South Devon

5   6
4   7
3   8   10   11   14
2   9   12   13
1

1. Torquay	8. Abbotsbury
2. Maidencombe	9. The Isle of Portland
3. Exmouth	10. Osmington Mills
4. Sidmouth	11. Lulworth Cove
5. Seaton	12. Kimmeridge
6. Lyme Regis	13. Swanage
7. West Bay	14. South Haven Point

The First Day

Torquay to Maidencombe: 7.3 miles, scenic rating 3.7

A generally wide path twists up and down through tall bushes, which yield views of the sea before the Path heads increasingly into woods. Well traveled by humans and dogs, the trail often is in residential areas, a situation conducive to litter.

Maidencombe is distinguished by two old thatched structures at the foot of its steep hill.

Above, a pub in lower Maidencombe. Left, just east of Torquay. Opposite, east of Sidmouth.

THINGS COULD BE WORSE

After the first day, as I get into bed, all seems well with the world.

But all is not well. In the dark of the morning, I get the chills and can't stop shaking. I put on my sweater and pullover, bury myself under my duvet, and break out in a hot sweat. I remove the duvet and shake from the chills. The cycle repeats. My pullover and sweater become sopping wet, so I take them off.

At 7:00 AM I call out to Steve, who is stirring in the room next to mine. He answers that he is awake. When I finally get him to enter my room, I moan from under the covers that death is within my grasp and would he please give me his duvet so I can be warmer.

The proprietress, Marianne, who had been a pharmacist for 40 years, takes charge. She moves me to a single room and arranges for a doctor in Torquay to pay a house call that afternoon.

Following our plan, Steve leaves. I eat lightly, watch some television, and nod off. There is a knock on my door. Marianne announces that the doctor has arrived. Instead, Eric Wallis, Secretary of the South West Coast Path Association, steps in.

"Just kidding about the doctor," he says. "I thought you needed some cheering up."

Then the real doctor, Nick Fisher, appears. With a sly grin, Nick says he has been waiting for years to get a sick American in his clutches. He tells me his secretary was sick during a visit to the United States and she spent a fortune in doctors' bills.

Nick assures me I will not die and prescribes medication, which Marianne gets at a nearby pharmacy. I spend another day at the Dartmoor Maiden Hotel in the care of two angels, Marianne and her housemaid.

Nick's bill is minimal. The medicine is free. Eric Wallis calls the next morning and insists on taking me to that day's B & B.

We walk a bit on the Path that afternoon. At the crest of a hill we look down on the village of Beer and on a line of colorful fishing boats beached on the shore. Beyond, high cliffs and bulging promontories mark the coastline.

It's a slow start for me, but there is no better place to be sick.

- Peter

The Second Day

<u>Maidencombe to Exmouth</u>: 11.4 miles, scenic rating 3.9

The Path skirts fields and passes through some thick woods on its way to Shaldon, where the ferry departs for Teignmouth. Leaving that busy town, walkers are on top of a seawall beside a rail line before they climb to a section part residential and part rural. Back at sea level, another long seawall route leads into and out of Dawlish, which is 2½ miles from Starcross, where the ferry runs to Exmouth.

Above, a harbor scene in Shaldon, where the ferry runs to Teignmouth. Steve waited here for his friend the Honorable Secretary of the SWCPA, who was waiting (correctly) on the other side.

Below, east of Maidencombe.

Top, east of the Otter Sanctuary flax is grown for linseed oil. Bottom, sea stacks near Ladram.

The Third Day

<u>Exmouth to Sidmouth</u>: 13.1 miles, scenic rating 4.4

Here is the medley of this section: 1. a long sea promenade 2. a wide grassy path by fields 3. a caravan park with about 5,000 caravans 4. a cliff path to Budleigh Salterton 5. a long sea promenade 6. the River Otter Sanctuary wetlands 7. fields and cliffs 8. fields, fewer cliffs, some woods, and another caravan park.

From number 4 above the Path is beautiful. Sidmouth is a Regency town with grand hotels on its hillside and along its esplanade.

THE TIP

In Sidmouth the B & Bs in the SWCP book are full, so I move up a notch and book at the Royal York and Faulkner Hotel.

After cleaning the mud off my boots outside, I push through the wooden revolving door and walk the soft carpet towards the front desk.

I glance left into the drawing room where some proper elderly ladies dressed in floral patterns are chatting over tea and cakes. The room is pale green with a recessed bay window that looks out over the sea. The furniture is Regency.

I glance to the right, peering into a large red-carpeted room where I will dine under cut glass chandeliers.

I think that the Royal York and Faulkner will live up to the hopes that its regal name inspires. The question is, will I live up to this hotel? As I near the front desk, I am conscious of my rain jacket and wet shorts.

A gentleman in a porter's gray uniform eyes me coldly. I'm not sure I hear him exactly, but I think he says, "What do **you** want?"

"I'm in off the Path," I explain, "and I have a room reserved."

"She'll help you," he says, indicating the receptionist behind the desk, and he leaves.

After checking in with the gentle receptionist, I ask her for help in the realm of tipping. My large pack, which was sent ahead by taxi, has been taken to my room. Should I tip the porter? She suggests one pound.

This is a one pound dilemma. If I tip the porter, am I rewarding surliness? Or am I showing Mr. Surly that I know how to behave even if he doesn't? Peter is sick in Maidencombe, not with me for advice.

For tea and cakes I wear my finest clothes: fairly clean jeans, running shoes, and a sweater with only a couple of small holes. I have a pound in my pocket, but the porter is not in.

Dinner that evening is superb, but I see no porter. The pound becomes an irritation.

The next morning I ask the receptionist if I can leave the tip for the porter with her. At that moment the porter arrives, but he is not the same man I had met. This one is taller, and he is happy to have the pound.

"It's been a wonderful stay," I tell the receptionist and the tall porter. "I've enjoyed it in every way."

- Steve

The Fourth Day

<u>Sidmouth to Seaton</u>: 10.4 miles, scenic rating 4.8

There are long, steep steps on this part of the Path, but also some trail for striding, often on a wide track with short-cropped grass. Pasture is more common than woods. Frequently there are precipitous views of the sea.

A drop takes the traveler into Branscombe, whose homes and cattle are in patches on the side of a long green valley.

Right, west of Branscombe and Weston Mouth. Below, at Beer, west of Seaton.

Above, Lyme Regis.
Below, Undercliffs National Nature Reserve.

The Fifth Day

<u>Seaton to Lyme Regis</u>: 6.8 miles, scenic rating 4.3

After a climb from Sidmouth and a walk through tall grasses, the traveler enters the woods of Undercliffs National Nature Reserve. On a wet day, it's slip, slide, and slop, and hope your nettle defense is effective. The woods are atmospherically thick. There are occasional sea views.

Lyme Regis is an old and large resort town situated on the sides of hills that slope to a well protected harbor.

The Sixth Day

<u>Lyme Regis to West Bay</u>: 9.7 miles, scenic rating 4.2 includes 5.0

      In 2002 land slippage has resulted in a lot of road walking between Lyme Regis and Charmouth (2.7 miles).

      After a climb from Charmouth, the Path is at its best. A lane leaving town rises steeply to farmland in a National Trust preserve at Stonebarrow and Golden Cap Estate. Golden Cap at 612 feet is the highest point on the south coast and offers panoramic views after a cliff-edge climb.

Above, climbing up Golden Cap from Seatown.
Below, the Path has a historic, cultural, and legal right-of-way through a farmer's fields near Seatown.

The Seventh Day

<u>West Bay to Abbotsbury</u>: 9.4 miles, scenic rating 4.6

This section has wide open views of long beaches and the sea. Inland there are caravan parks, golf courses, and residential areas mixed in with the fields. Much of this walking is on wide grassy carpet.

The Path drops to holiday coves and levels out going into West Bexington. From there it climbs to a high ridge with excellent views. The last miles into Abbotsbury are exhilarating.

Abbotsbury is a lovely old village.

Left, St. Catherine's Chapel on Chapel Hill above Abbotsbury. It was part of a monastery dissolved by Henry VIII in 1543.
Above, east of West Bay.

The Eighth Day

<u>Abbotsbury to Osmington Mills, Inland Route</u>: 13.8 miles, scenic rating 4.9

A narrow lane from Abbotsbury climbs to a ridge where walkers survey sloping pastures and the sea far away. Sheep bleat across the valleys.

After the Hardy Monument, 3 miles on, the valleys become broader, and villages appear in the distance. Tumuli and other ancient remains are common.

The thirteenth-century Smugglers Inn is nestled between low hills near the cove at Osmington Mills.

Above, the hang glider will land on the hillside in the foreground. Osmington is in the background. Right, Sutton Poyntz, which is near Osmington, is in the background. Opposite, on a hillside above Abbotsbury.

COWS

Today on a hillside above Abbotsbury I discover that cows are curious. I take a photo of a bunch of them, run out of shots on that roll, and move to a fence about 10 yards away to change film. In the middle of that procedure a cow comes over to see what I'm doing.

"Sorry, no food," I explain politely.

The cow noses me as a friend of hers joins us.

"No food," I repeat.

A third cow joins us, and cow # 1 moves her nose towards my pack, which is on the ground.

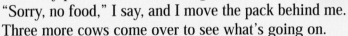

"Sorry, no food," I say, and I move the pack behind me.

Three more cows come over to see what's going on.

I offer the back of my hand to the first three, and one of them gives me a lick, but clearly none of them are there for free licks, any more than the next 3 that push in. In case you haven't been counting, 9 cows are now watching me change film.

At last that job is done. I lean back and try to photograph the ladies, but they are so close, I get only 2 or 3 noses in the frame.

It's time to move up to a gate I have avoided. I hoped I would not have to climb over it because at least 12 cows are on the other side, but by now I know the Path continues through those cows.

The cows there are in a lane with a fence on each side. As I climb up and straddle the gate, I raise my voice in reassuring tones to the crowd.

"Good morning, ladies. I won't hurt you. I just need to pass through on the left side. That would be your right."

Pausing to talk is a bad idea. There are about 40 other cows farther down the lane, and as soon as a few see and hear me up on the gate, they look at me as alertly as is possible for a cow, and drift my way to see what's going on. As they come on, other cows are alerted, and soon all 40 plus the 12 originals look up at me curiously.

Ten minutes later after a lot of smooth talk and some hesitant butt-patting, I pass the last cow. A procession of cows and a chorus of moos follow me down the lane.

- Steve

NOW I UNDERSTAND

The English and Yanks don't speak exactly the same language. A British friend once told me I might have klonked my elbow, but I certainly didn't bonk it. He urged me to wear a waist pack, not a fanny pack. I had been talking dirty.

Today I am waiting for a bus on the Isle of Portland. I need to get back to Weymouth by 2:00 PM to catch the bus to Osmington Mills.

My timing is perfect. A bus rounds the curve and careens in my direction. The bus signals left to pick me up, and I give it a cheerful wave, as if to say, "Yes, you clever bus, I do want a ride."

The bus veers right, speeds up, and leaves me staring at its rear end.

"Wait!" I cry.

I am in shorts and running shoes. I take off.

I fly down the street. The wind lifts my hair.

100 yards. 200 yards. Pick up the pace. Fly!

I'm keeping the bus in sight.

Spectators cheer me on, the old guy chasing the bus.

"Catch him, mate! Get 'im!"

I can still see the bus. Don't let up!

The bus signals left and slows. It's stopping.

I race into the bus stop, approaching a young lady, who I hope is about to board. I yell, "Stop the bus!"

My momentum carries me past the young lady, who looks mildly surprised as I sail by. I let her get on before me.

I am breathing hard and my eyes are wild.

"What was wrong with that bus stop back there?" I ask the driver, jerking my thumb in the direction.

"You waved me off," the driver says firmly. "That means you don't want me to stop."

"Oh!" I say. I laugh. "Oh, my."

I arrive on time in Weymouth, where the driver and I part on good terms. I am a step closer to proper communication in England.

- Steve

The Ninth Day

<u>The Isle of Portland</u>: 8.5 miles with bus ride, scenic rating 4.8

　　To avoid a long busy causeway, take a bus from Weymouth to "the heights," then proceed south on the sidewalk about 100 yards to the footpath. You can go east or west.

　　Old but active military sites and stone quarries are numerous on the heights. There are spectacular views east, south, and west, especially to the west from a high cliff. The island slopes gently to the Bill, its exposed and grassy southern tip, where a lighthouse stands.

Above, the old harbor in Weymouth. The town, on the official Path route, welcomes tourists with clear signs, information booths, and clean streets, some closed to traffic. Below, on the southern end of the Isle of Portland, also on the official Path route.

Above, west of Lulworth Cove.
Opposite, closer to the cove, the arch called Durdle Door.
Below, the last climb before the descent to Lulworth Cove.

The Tenth Day

<u>Osmington Mills to Lulworth Cove</u>: 6.5 miles, scenic rating 4.9

After 2 miles of walking through low pasture, hikers climb to spectacular terrain. The Path has roller-coaster sections at great heights on the grassy edge of weaving white limestone cliffs plunging to the sea. The walkway is soft. The last mile is stepped and busy.

Lulworth Cove is a one-lane beach village with a heritage center to one side. It is apt to be busy with visitors. Not far up the road, West Lulworth is another worthy possibility for lodging and dining.

RESPONSE

 Sometimes I like a British response.

 Not for the first time today, I descend 100 steep steps down a hillside, noticing that the Path on the opposite hill has 100 equally steep steps going back up.

 "I think we're going all the way down again," I say to a bloke who is descending with me. "Who made this Path?"

 "God," he replies with a slight smile.

 "Indeed," I say. "By the way, do you know how far it is to Lulworth Cove? I'm hoping to see some of the match on television there."

 "You should be there in about an hour," he says.

 "Then I might make it," I say. "I wouldn't be late if I hadn't stopped for so many photos."

 "It's a weekend," he says. "You can't be late."

 "Quite so," I reply.

- Steve

Top, the army ranges seen from the Lulworth Cove end. Bottom, the ranges from the Kimmeridge end.
Opposite, top: looking back after a climb from Kimmeridge. Opposite, bottom: St. Aldhelm's Head, a further climb to the east.

The Eleventh Day

<u>Lulworth Cove to Kimmeridge</u>: 7.3 miles, scenic rating 5.0

This section on the edge of the army firing ranges follows the cliff tops with fine seaward and inland views. Check the SWCP Guide to see when the Path here is open. If it is closed, the inland range road might be open and save hikers a long walk around.

The thatched homes of Kimmeridge are made of the local brown-gray stone common in villages in this area.

The Twelfth Day

<u>Kimmeridge to Swanage</u>: 13.3 miles, scenic rating 4.8

As far as the lighthouse outside Swanage, walkers generally are on the edge of cliffs. The Path first is gently rolling, then has severe climbing, and then is easy again after St. Aldhelm's Head. The footing always is comfortable. There are two inland loops.

Swanage is large, busy, and cheerfully touristy. It has many fine buildings and attractions.

Hikers view Old Harry Rocks, top, and then Knoll Beach, bottom, on the way to South Haven Point.

The Thirteenth Day

<u>Swanage to Sandbanks Ferry at South Haven Point</u>: 7.6 miles, scenic rating 4.5

By fields, by sea, and along firm-packed beach, the Path reaches its end. The route is heavily traveled. Some walkers might consider the Heath Nature Preserve in the dunes a better attraction than the naturist (nudist) section of the beach.

The village of Studland, worth a visit, is just off the Path.

CELEBRATION

On my last day of walking the Path, how can I express my feelings? I started this trek five years ago. These are the last fields, the last high sea walks, and the last beaches. Five years!

I move in weightless surprise. The moment. Here and now.

I will have someone take my picture at the sign. What will it say? Minehead 630 miles, with an arrow. The British are understated.

I see the ferry at the finish. I come closer. I don't see the sign. I reach the sidewalk at the ferry. No sign is anywhere.

"Are you Coast Path people?" I ask two guys with a map.

"Sort of," one says with a cautious smile.

"Is this the end?" I ask.

They unfold the map. The green Coast Path line stops where we are standing.

"I think it is," the other says.

"I've come from Minehead," I say. "Isn't there a band? Fireworks? A celebration?"

Their wives join us. They ask questions I like. How long has it taken? How did I find out about the Coast Path? Peter's name enters the conversation.

One wife says they are from Devon.

"Peter has a daughter whose father-in-law lives in Devon. We'll stay there for a couple of nights," I say.

"What part of Devon?"

"Near Totnes."

"We're Totnes!"

"Have you heard of a little village called Harberton?" I ask.

"We're Harberton!" they exclaim. "Who are you staying with?"

"They're fairly new there. Ro and Sue Barkas."

"Ro and Sue!" one wife exclaims. "Their upper window looks into my bathroom!"

"We're all friends!"

This moment is my celebration.

- Steve

An impressive marker was in place a few months after this meeting.

Right, at the start of their sixth year Peter and Steve pose beside the new marker at South Haven Point, which celebrates the official finish/start of the Coast Path. The marker was unveiled on May 12, 2003. An impressive sculpture at Minehead, unveiled February 14, 2001, marks the start/finish of the Path.
Below, south of Bude.

FROM THIS POINT

In year six we return to attend to some details of this book. With health restored, I finally get to South Haven Point.

Memories flood my mind – of spectacular cliff-side scenery, steep green hills to climb, stream-fed combes, fishing villages tucked into the hillsides, and, of course, recurrent signs of England's deep history.

I treasure the comradery with Steve, the countless acts of kindness shown to us, and the sheer joy of it all. This is an experience to share with others.

- Peter

Above, Peter is lost in thought at the mouth of the River Erme, before Bigbury-on-Sea. Below, at Corfe.

PART TWO

Planning Your Walk

THE ESSENTIALS

GUIDEBOOKS If you are going to walk the Path for more than a day or two, you will want guidebooks. We used the ones below.

1. *The South West Coast Path Guide*, published and written by the South West Coast Path Association is **the essential guide**. Their excellent Web site is at www.swcp.org.uk. Their administrator, who welcomes inquiries, is Liz Wallis, at Windlestraw, Penquit, Ermington, Devon, PL21 OLU; tel./fax 01752 896237.

Above, the essentials go over a stile near Trevone. Opposite, near Bude Steve should have used the guidebook. Previous page: The Rumps, west of Port Isaac.

The guide includes trail descriptions, distances, levels of difficulty, member-approved accommodations, transportation information, tourist centers, youth hostels, camp sites, tide tables, river crossing information, and more. A reverse guide (Poole to Minehead) is available as a supplement.

2. *South West Coast Path Association Path Descriptions.* These 45 pamphlets are in greater detail than the Guide and include maps.

3. *National Trail Guides.* These books use Ordnance Survey maps, which show roads and details a mile or more inland. The guides include a great deal of history, points of interest, and fine photographs. The Coast Path series has four volumes: Minehead to Padstow, Padstow to Falmouth, Falmouth to Exmouth, and Exmouth to Poole.

4. *The Rough Guide to Devon & Cornwall* by Robert Andrews. These 338 pages include a substantial amount of material on the coast.

To order guidebooks, see our Web sites section or the SWCP Guide.

THE SLIPPERY SLOPE

On a cliff top past Bude, I follow the orange arrow that often marks the Coast Path, but find myself heading inland, so I cut across a field to look for the Coast Path closer to the sea.

Sure enough, I come to a gate where I see the Path winding around the headland on the other side of a steep valley. The vegetation on the valley slope looks short and smooth.

After I head down the slope, the vegetation becomes a little higher. I pass through some brambles, which become waist high, but I get only a scratch or two on my bare legs.

Some other vegetation appears with thorns an inch long. When there is nothing except this growth to walk on, I manage to stay on top, only occasionally falling part way through. My legs are not bleeding badly.

I think about going back, but a return would be up a long, steep hill, full of brambles. I take out a rain coat to shield one hand and rain pants for the other. These defenses are good, but not perfect.

I try to find thick branches down in the thorns for support. Foot down. Ouch. Foot up. Ouch! Take care not to pitch forward. Ouch.

By now going back clearly is no better than pressing on, even though I am wondering how my death will come. Will I fall through over my head and be stuck until I starve? Will I bleed to death?

If I could get over there – ouch! And there – ouch! I slide into a muddy, overgrown stream bed, take a photo, and climb back up. A few more brambles and stinging nettle – ouch, ouch, ouch! – and I'm out.

Now I know the manner of my death. I will die from acute embarrassment as soon as someone sees my lacerated legs.

- Steve

MORE ESSENTIALS

BASE LODGING   We like the adventure and continuity of the inn-to-inn walk, but some people prefer to have a home base, perhaps in a self-catering unit, which includes a kitchen. These walkers often take public transportation to a starting point and then walk back to their base or car.

TRANSPORTATION   Trains and buses run from the major airports to the coast. Buses sometimes are available between coastal villages. Read their complicated schedules carefully.

　　If someone in your group dares to drive the one-lane roads, check ahead to see where you should park in the village you hope to visit.

KIT TRANSFER   For carefree comfort have your pack taken to the next lodging by taxi or friend. Some proprietors will offer this service for a fee. Ask them, or look for KT (kit transfer) in the SWCP Guide. The cost of sending our packs ahead by taxi was about £14.00, or $20.00, on average. The cost is regardless of the number of packs being sent.

WHAT TO BRING
1. Sun protection.
2. Rain gear, waterproof boots, and a wind parka.
3. We hiked in June. We often got down to a T-shirt, but then were apt to put on another layer or two as we cooled off at lunch break. Three layers plus the parka were sufficient.
4. Carry plenty of water. Most of the Coast Path is in the open.
5. Shorts. You don't mind a little stinging nettle, do you?

Left, a steep climb near Southdown Cliffs and Sharkham Point, west of Brixham. Opposite, Peter has brought everything he needs, near Prussia Cove.

6. Blister remedy. You shouldn't need a big first aid kit, but deal promptly with blisters. Break in new boots before the trip.

7. A light day pack if you are sending your luggage ahead by taxi or friend, but be prepared for the rare occasion when you will want to carry your belongings a short distance to avoid a huge fare. These occasions arise when you need to cross a river, and the route for the taxi is long, but you can use a pedestrian ferry, and meet a taxi on the other side of the river.

8. NO BUG REPELLENT IS NEEDED! Do the British coming to America know about mosquitoes and other man-eating insects? They might be in for a surprise.

9. Peter loves a hiking stick.

10. Steve loves long-sleeved polypro shirts.

TRAIL TIPS

1. The South West Coast Path generally has very good footing. It has level stretches, but often goes up and down. The South West Coast Path Association calculates that in the course of its 630 miles the Path climbs over 91,000 feet, more than three Everests. But don't worry. That's less than 150 feet per mile.

2. Hikers range in age from 2 to 90 (or less, or more!), but all hikers should be in reasonably good condition before setting out on a walk of any significant distance. The South West Coast Path Guide gives distances and difficulty ratings of easy, moderate, strenuous, and severe.

3. If you bring a dog, a leash will be required when livestock are on the trail. You will be expected to use a scooper and bag for any droppings. Receptacles are provided.

4. We favor including a layover day each week. We used ours for relaxing and doing laundry, but it was available also in case of horrible weather.

Our taxi arrives at the foot of the manor house lane in Place.

5. Allow plenty of time for taking photos, talking to other walkers, and hiking to points of interest.

6. The SWCPA encourages membership in the 5-a-Day Club. Members pick up 5 pieces of litter each day. For this club there are no fees, no mail, and no recognition.

WHEN TO GO

The middle of May is the best time to see wild flowers, but they appear in April and are still beautiful in June. September and October are also beautiful months on the Path. Some hardy souls like the bleak and stormy weather of winter.

July and August have the warmest and the driest weather, but they also have the greatest crowds. B & Bs fill up. Traffic jams on the narrow roads can occur.

Maintenance of the trail improves after May.

PLODDING THE PATH

An occasional brute will shoulder a fifty-pound pack and gallop along the trail at over twenty miles a day. Some people think there is a better way.

Giving up the satisfaction of being Ironman triathletes, they enjoy the views at a leisurely pace.

Sally, who brings her black lab on the Path, says, "This is my Valium."

Michael from London, who brings his girlfriend and likes to explore antiquities, says, "It's to be plodded, this Path."

Lizzie fields questions for the South West Coast Path Association and says of one racer, "I should have been sharp with him. You must slow down if you want to see more than your boots."

An unhurried pace is the reason Rent-a-Dog shops flourish along the Path. If you want to look and act like a native, you can rent almost any breed, leashed and trained to stroll. (Contact dogs-r-us@notreally.com.)

Above, Sally and her lab relax at a spot south of St. Agnes.
Left, above Seatown.

This spry gentleman and his friend passed us on the cliffs south of Gurnard's Head. Below, from the cliffs south of Gurnard's Head.

MR. SPRY

Beyond Mussel Point we meet a sprightly man ten years our elder. He is leading a young friend, going from Treen to St. Ives for lunch. We will be spending the entire day going the same distance.

Mr. Spry lets slip that he sometimes hikes the Path from Land's End to St. Ives in one day, a distance of about 24 miles that we plan to cover in three days. He acknowledges that his wife thinks he's a bit daft.

The young lady with him is not his wife, but might have the same opinion she has. This companion says she will take a taxi from St. Ives back to her hotel, a return trip that Mr. Spry plans to walk that afternoon.

BIRDING, ROCKS, AND FLOWERS

The Cornwall Bird Watching and Preservation Society is up in the air in 2003. Inquire at a Tourist Information Centre to contact them.

The Devon Bird Watching & Preservation Society can be found on the Web. Their site will give upcoming events and helpful people to contact.

There are many opportunities for bird watching along the Coast Path. For example, west of Boscastle, the Long and Short Islands are sanctuaries for breeding seabirds, including the largest colony of puffins in Cornwall. Consider also the River Otter Sanctuary near Budleigh Salterton, the Camel Estuary at

At The Swannery in Abbotsbury.

Padstow and Polzeath, the Hayle Estuary, Helford, Land's End, The Lizard, Prawle Point, and Start Point.

Walk the Cornish Coastal Path by John Mason, published by Collins, has two pages of valuable information on birding.

That book also has information on geology, animal life, and plants and flowers. The author recommends the Geological Museum in Penzance, as well as the Morrab Gardens there.

If you travel by car, the botanical gardens of the Eden Project in St. Austell, not far from Mevagissey, are drawing very large crowds.

The geology of the coast between Exmouth and Swanage is of special interest. Contact the Tourist Information Centres listed in the SWCPA guidebook and/or visit www.jurassiccoast.com.

I'm searching for flowers -
   The bloody cranesbill,
The pillwort, the dropwort,
   Abundant spring squill -
I'm searching for flowers
   Especially rare -
The dog rose, tormentil,
   And pygmy rush fair,
Black bog-rush,
   Thyme broomrape,
And Bobington's leek,
   The lowly mock grape
And harebells I seek -
   There's bachelor's buttons,
Codlins-and-cream,
   Restharrow, tamfuzz,
And tab mawn supreme -
   I pray I'll be lucky
And stumble across
   Green-winged orchid,
Or viper's bugloss -
   For kidney vetch, quillet,
Dodder and more
   Are flowers of Cornwall
I adore.

                          -Steve

An impostor has slipped into this poem. Who would suspect the lowly mock grape? If you spotted this intruder into the world of real Cornish flowers and plants, you are an expert.

BRIDS-FIT TRIFFLE

A few feet off the Path below me two young men are bending over, searching in the grass. They are lifting some plant leaves gently to examine them, then moving on, pointing and chatting.

Above, the trefoil hunters search for the rare flower in a spot past Fowey. Opposite, poppy and common winter cress near Portscatho.

I stop. "What are you finding?" I ask.

"The rare brid fit triffle," one replies. "It's hard to recognize after a year away," the other adds.

"Would I disturb you or the plants if I took a look?" I ask.

"Not at all. Come on down."

The quarry seems to be a small, delicate yellow flower. I keep my boots clear of them.

"It likes an unfertilized slope like this, not cropped, and not alkaline. Ah. We might have one here."

He points, then lifts a tender stem. I settle in beside him.

"It's a smaller flower than the other trefoil you see," he explains, "and pure yellow, not with the touch of orange." He is still examining. "Also, it has a longer seed stem. I'm not sure about this one."

I stare at the small, cupped flower. "I don't think I see the seed stem," I say.

"This is it," he says, indicating something that looks like a long, green thorn.

I glance to the side. "Is this one?" I ask. I lift a small yellow flower with a longer seed stem than the one he has shown me.

"A fantastic one," he says. "That's clearly a bird's-foot."

I stand. "Thank you," I say. "Thanks for inviting me into this world."

I have found the rare bird's-foot trefoil.

- Steve

THE WEATHER

During five years of hiking we endured some sea mist, an occasional sprinkle, and a half hour of rain. More rain is normal.

- An old adage: If you can see Lundy Island, it's going to rain.
  If you can't see Lundy Island, it <u>is</u> raining.

- From a walker/runner who completed the entire Path in 23 days: "We had continuing and showering rain with gale force head winds for the first fifteen days and blistering heat towards the end."

- From a walker who completed the Path over 6 years: "Two maxims: there is no such thing as 'waterproof' and always walk towards a hot shower."

Government rain stations at Bude on Cornwall's Atlantic coast and at Exeter in Devon near the English Channel show the least rainfall from April through July. Rainfall amounts are greatest at Bude from October through January. It rains the most at Exeter in December and January.

MACKEREL SKIES

"Lovely day," I say to a gent on a bench overlooking a blue sea.

"It won't last," he retorts.

The gentleman casts a practiced eye to a sky turning slightly cloudy. "Mackerel skies and mares' tails make tall ships carry small sails," he says with a rueful smile.

"Does that mean a storm is coming?" I ask.

"I'm afraid so," he says.

"Does it really rain for two weeks at a time?" I persist.

The man's eyes light up.

"Oh, yes," he says. "It can do that."

Above, Steve battles wind south of Portreath. Opposite, below Golden Cap.

The locals believe in a net sum of awful days, and that sum is enough to float Noah's Ark.

After a sunny spell we foreign travelers are like Romanized Celts hearing rumors of howling, naked, long-haired hordes painted blue (Angles and Saxons by name) who mean the Celts no good. But instead of Angles and Saxons, we hear about Bad Weather.

As we approach our final destination for the year, we are anxious. After weeks of walking the Path, we have had a half hour of rain, a little drizzle, and some mist. Can you imagine the coming deluge?

- Steve

PLANNING
LEISURELY WALKS

This part of the book covers these seven sections of the Path.

"You must not rush the Path," one walker told us.

In the following pages we break seven beautiful sections of the Path into small pieces so that travelers can plan leisurely walks. Every village we name has lodging, which is listed either in our Recommended Lodging section or in the SWCP Guide.

For walkers who like to spend extra time in one area, we tell about our top points of interest near or on the Path, and we refer to lovely circle walks that take the hiker inland, but often include a part of the Path.

Villages and towns suitable for an extended layover are **in bold**. Accommodations in those places often include cottages with kitchens.

SECTION ONE: LORNA DOONE COUNTRY

There are steep slopes, weathered cliffs, farms, lush valleys, and invigorating hill climbs in this stretch of multi-textured land.

Above, signs request that no stones be thrown in the harbor at Porlock Weir.

Minehead to Woolacombe: 49 miles, pages 15-20 in Part One
Minehead – West Lynch/Bossington (7 miles) – Porlock (2 miles) –
Porlock Weir (2 miles) – Silcombe (4 miles) – Countisbury (5 miles) –
Lynmouth/Lynton (3 miles) – Heddon Valley (7 miles) – Combe Martin
(6 miles) – **Ilfracombe** (6 miles) – Lee (3 Miles) – **Mortehoe/
Woolacombe** (4 miles)

Top attractions: Lundy Island, which can be reached from Ilfracombe, has
seals, excellent birding in spring and early summer, a thirteenth-century
castle, and dramatic cliff scenery.
        Lynmouth has a water-powered cliff railway on a sheer drop.
        Also recommended: Culbone Church near Porlock (see pages 17,
163), Valley of the Rocks near Lynton (pages 19, 165), Hunters Inn in
Heddon Valley (page 19), and Great Hangman near Combe Martin (page
19).

Circle walks are at Minehead, Porlock Weir, Lynmouth, Combe Martin,
Ilfracombe, and Mortehoe. To investigate circle trips, see resources on pages
174-180.

SECTION TWO: LAND OF KING ARTHUR AND THOMAS HARDY

Sweeping pastoral views and rugged cliff-top scenery are mixed with dense woods and surfing beaches. The hiker sees bulging headlands, rocky coves, steep hills, and narrow valleys.

Buck's Mills to Tintagel: 48 miles, pages 24-35 in Part One
Buck's Mills – **Clovelly** (4 miles) – Gawlish (6 miles) – Hartland Quay (4 miles) – Morwenstow (8 miles) – Bude (8 miles) – Crackington Haven (6 miles) – **Boscastle** (7 miles) – Tintagel/Bossiney (5 miles)
Tintagel to Newquay: 48 miles, pages 35-39
Tintagel – Trebarwith (3 miles) – Portgaverne (7 miles) – Port Isaac (1 mile) – Polzeath (9 miles) – **Padstow** (3 miles) – Trevone (6 miles) – Constantine Bay (5 miles) – Treyarnon (1 mile) – Mawgan Porth (7 miles) – **Newquay** (6 miles)

Top attractions: Hartland Abbey lies about two miles east of Hartland Quay. Henry VIII gave the abbey to his wine steward, whose descendants have owned it ever since. Their portraits, spanning over 400 years, hang on the

Above, Peter strikes a pose at High Cliff. Opposite, the stream at Boscastle runs to a narrow harbor protected by a high wharf.

walls of the abbey's rooms. The current version of this medieval abbey was finished in 1779.

South of Crackington Haven is High Cliff, which at 700 feet is the highest point in Cornwall.

A rustic path leads from Boscastle to the country church of St. Julitta at Hennett where Thomas Hardy wooed and won the rector's blue-eyed sister-in-law. They lived unhappily ever after.

Bedruthan Steps, giant rock stacks, rise from the beach north of Mawgan Porth.

Also recommended: Clovelly (pages 24, 25), Hartland Quay (page 26), Morwenstow (pages 27, 163, 169), Prideaux Place in Padstow (page 36), The Rumps near Polzeath (pages 36, 37), St. Enodoc Church near Port Isaac (page 37), and Tintagel Castle (page 33).

Circle walks are at Buck's Mills, Clovelly, Hartland Quay, Morwenstow, Bude, Crackington Haven, Boscastle, Tintagel, Port Isaac, and Padstow.

SECTION THREE: RUINED MINES ABOVE THE SEA

To Gwithian towering cliffs and small coves mark a barren landscape made eerie by the remnants of the tin mining industry.

Past St. Ives slopes of scrubby grass with scattered rock outcrops drop to the sea. Inland, stone walls create a patchwork of fields. More tin mining ruins follow, and then past Land's End high cliffs dominate a jagged coast.

Newquay to Gwithian: 29 miles, pages 39-43 in Part One
Newquay – Holywell/Cubert (4 miles, using ferry or footbridge after Newquay) – Perranporth (5 miles) – **St. Agnes** (4 miles) – Porthtowan (5 miles) – Portreath (4 miles) – Gwithian/Hayle (7 miles)
St. Ives to Porthcurno: 30 miles, pages 43-50
St. Ives – Zennor (8 miles) – Treen (2 miles) – Botallack (6 miles) – **Sennen** (7 miles) – Land's End (2 miles) – Porthcurno (5 miles)

Top attractions: Perran Beach at Perranporth is a surfing beach three miles long. Hang gliders circle to the beach from the heights of the sandstone cliffs.

Above, Greeb Cottage at Land's End. Below, tin mining ruins north of St. Agnes. Opposite, Perran Beach at Perranporth.

Not far past Perranporth there is a restored engine house at Blue Hills Tin Streams where volunteers demonstrate the tinner's craft of "vanning, panning, and jigging."

Past Treen the lighthouse at Pendeen Watch is open to the public.

The National Trust runs a tin mining museum at the Geevor Tin Mine Heritage Centre near Botallack.

At Land's End Greeb Cottage depicts the hard life of a farm family on that windswept peninsula in the eighteenth century.

Also recommended: Zennor Quoit (page 124), the mermaid carving in Zennor church, and the Minack Theatre at Porthcurno (page 50).

Circle walks are at Perranporth, St. Agnes, Portreath, Treen, Botallack, Sennen, and Porthcurno.

QUOITING

Our maps often show a line of small x marks, which indicate a Neolithic cliff castle with ramparts.

But when we arrive at a Neolithic castle site, the castle generally looks like a sheep pasture. One Neolithic castle site looked like a putting green.

I love Neolithic castles and ramparts, so on the day the guide book describes a Neolithic communal tomb with actual stones a mere 1¼ miles off the Path at Zennor, I hurry to see it. The Neolithic arrangement of stones I am looking for is called the Zennor Quoit.

The local who runs the village pub gives directions to the trail.

"How far up is the quoit?" I ask.

"Oh, I've never been there," the man says.

The trail is about where he said it would be. In a few hundred yards it disappears, but I pick it up again heading up a knoll which is covered on top with massive boulders stacked like pancakes to form the walls of small chambers.

I wonder how Neolithic man moved the huge stones, almost as large as those at Stonehenge. I take photos.

I move on to a high stone that has a large bowl scooped out for some mysterious Neolithic reason. The presence of ancestral man is thick in the air. I take more photos.

I meet Mick and Dave, also quoiting.

"What do you think?" I ask. "Are these the quoits?"

"Zennor Quoit might be over there," Mick says. He points to a small bump in the distance. "These would seem to be natural formations."

I have taken twenty shots of natural nothings.

The brothers and I head for the possible quoit. Skirting barbed wire is a challenge, but in less than an hour we reach a block of massive stones.

"A farmer last century pulled the roof down," Mick says, "but a vicar paid him 30 shillings to stop the destruction."

I crawl inside, stepping on the dead of 5,000 years ago. The place is older than Stonehenge, and at Stonehenge you have to organize a riot and assault to get closer than 20 yards.

I emerge and take photos.

"Look over there," Dave says.

A tiny bump is on the horizon.

"It's the Lanyon Quoit," Dave says.

"It counts," I say.

In one day I have bagged two quoits.

- Steve

Left, Hell Stone Cromlech is off the Path, hard to find, past Abbotsbury. Opposite, Mick and Dave in front of the Zennor Quoit, which is in the left of the photo. A cromlech is a quoit. They are Neolithic tombs.

SECTION FOUR: CORNWALL'S GENTLE SOUTH COAST

Unlike Cornwall's rugged north coast, the south coast has gently sloping hills carpeted in lush grass. Many of the hills rise to great heights above valleys with clear streams. There are coves, pocket beaches, and subtropical flora. On the great peninsula called The Lizard formations of schist and serpentine create a craggy shoreline.

At Vellan Head, near Lizard Point.

Porthcurno to Church Cove: 42 miles, pages 50-56 in Part One Porthcurno – St. Loy Cove (3 miles) – Lamorna (3 miles) – Mousehole (3 miles) – Newlyn (2 miles) – **Penzance** (1 mile) – Marazion (4 miles) – Perranuthnoe (2 miles) – Praa Sands (4 miles) – Porthleven (4 miles) – Gunwalloe (4 miles) – Mullion Cove (3 miles) – The Lizard (7 miles) – Housel Bay (1 mile) – Church Cove (1 mile)
Church Cove to Falmouth: 32 miles, pages 56-60
Church Cove – Cadgwith/Ruan Minor (2 miles) – Coverack (7 miles) – Porthallow (3 miles) – Gillan (3 miles) – Manaccan (3 miles) – **Helford** (4 miles) – Mawnan Smith (4 miles) – **Falmouth** (6 miles)

Top attractions: In Newlyn the Pilchard Works is a working museum devoted to Cornwall fishing.

At Marazion St. Michael's Mount is Cornwall's version of Mont Saint Michel in France.

Past Porthleven a shaded dirt road leads two miles along Loe Pool, Cornwall's largest natural lake, to Penrose Estate, whose pastoral grounds

On the road into Cadgwith.

are open to the public.

     At Gunwalloe (Church Cove, Gunwalloe) isolated, fourteenth-century St. Winwaloe Church has survived centuries of storms, sea surges, and sweeping dunes. It is partially buried.

     Across from Helford the 25 acres of Trebah Gardens cascade down a wooded valley to the Helford River.

     The National Maritime Museum is in Falmouth.

     Also recommended: Frenchman's Creek near Helford (pages 58-59) and Logan Rock near Porthcurno (pages 51, 157).

     <u>Circle walks</u> are at Porthcurno, Lamorna, Perranuthnoe, Praa Sands, Porthleven, Mullion Cove, The Lizard, Housel Bay, Cadgwith, Coverack, Porthallow, Helford, Mawnan Smith, and Falmouth.

Above, Portloe. Below, a ferry stops at the bottom of this lane in Fowey and crosses the river to Bodinnick. There the beautiful Hall Walk leads to Polruan, where a ferry returns walkers to Fowey.

SECTION FIVE: CORNISH FISHING VILLAGES

Green headlands, rolling hills, fields dotted with sheep or cows, and fishing villages tucked into narrow rocky coves typify this section. Many of these communities are the favorite spots of artists, who know that around every corner a picture is waiting to be painted.

Steve on the Path in Cawsand.

St. Mawes to Fowey: 44 miles, pages 60-68 in Part One
St. Mawes – Portscatho (6 miles) – Pendower Beach (3 miles) – Portloe (5 miles) – **Gorran Haven** (9 miles) – **Mevagissey** (4 miles) – Charlestown (7 miles) – Carlyon Bay (2 miles) – Par (2 miles) – **Fowey** (6 miles)

Fowey to Plymouth: 34 miles, pages 68-74
Fowey/Polruan – **Polperro** (7 miles) – Looe (5 miles) – Portwrinkle (8 miles) – Lower Tregantle (2 miles) – Cawsand/Kingsand (9 miles) – **Plymouth** (3 miles)

Top attractions: Near Gorran Haven a massive headland called Dodman Point is home to Exmoor ponies, imported by the National Trust to crop the gorse on The Dodman's slopes.

Close to the Path in Cremyll, across from Plymouth, Mount Edgcumbe Mansion has grounds that slope to the water's edge. The sixteenth-century home was restored after being firebombed in World War II. The mansion, its grounds, and its gardens are open to the public.

Also recommended: The Gribbin, east of Par (page 68), the Hall Walk near Fowey (page 68), and Rame Head, west of Cawsand (pages 72-73).

Circle walks are at St. Mawes, Portscatho, Pendower Beach, Portloe, Gorran Haven, Mevagissey, Fowey, Polperro, Looe, and Cawsand.

SECTION SIX: DEVON'S SOUTH HAMS AND TORBAY COASTLINE

Britain's mildest climate holds sway in this area, where subtropical flora flourish. Hams means sheltered place. In this verdant setting cliff-top scenery along a rocky coastline is broken by estuaries, snug harbors, and some lowlands.

Newton Ferrers to Torcross: 41 miles, pages 74-79 in Part One
Newton Ferrers/Noss Mayo – River Erme (9 miles) – Bigbury-on-Sea (5 miles) – Thurlestone (3 miles) – Hope Cove (3 miles) – Soar (4 miles) – **Salcombe** (4 miles) – Rudder Cove (2 miles) – Start Point (7 miles) – Beesands/Beeson (2 miles) – Torcross (2 miles)
Torcross to Maidencombe: 35 miles, pages 79-83
Torcross – **Dartmouth** (11 miles, includes 5 by bus from Strete) – Kingswear (1 mile) – Brixham (8 miles) – **Torquay** (8 miles) – Maidencombe (7 miles)

Top attractions: The estuary of the River Erme is unspoiled.

At high tide a sea tractor runs to Burgh Island from Bigbury-on-Sea. At low tide visitors to the island can walk across the sands.

The lighthouse at Start Point is open to the public.

East of Dartmouth are the subtropical gardens of Coleton Fishacre, dropping towards the sea on lovely grounds.

Near Torquay, Cockington is a showcase village with many of its buildings open to the public. Some of the buildings are from the Middle Ages. The grounds are spacious. The distance to the village from the Path is about a mile, on path or by road.

Circle walks are at Newton Ferrers, Bigbury-on-Sea, Salcombe, and Dartmouth.

Above, the lighthouse at Start Point was built in 1886. Below, near Bigbury-on-Sea. Opposite, Peter approaches Prawl Point, between Salcombe and Beesands.

Visitors enter Corfe Castle through its thirteenth-century outer gate.

SECTION SEVEN: SOUTH COAST, EAST DEVON, AND DORSET

This stretch of the Coast Path, the Jurassic Coast, is a World Heritage Site representing 185 million years of earth history. It offers towering green-carpeted cliffs, pebbled beaches, and bays carved out of bands of limestone.

<u>Sidmouth to Osmington Mills</u>: 51 miles, pages 88-93 in Part One
Sidmouth – Branscombe (4 miles) – **Beer** (4 miles) – Seaton (2 miles) – **Lyme Regis** (8 miles) – Seatown/Axmouth (7 miles) – Bridport/West Bay (3 miles) – Burton Bradstock (2 miles) – West Bexington (4 miles) – **Abbotsbury** (7 miles) – Osmington Mills (10 miles)
<u>Osmington Mills to Studland</u>: 33 miles, pages 93-100
Osmington Mills – West Lulworth (6 miles) – Kimmeridge (8 miles) – Kingston (8 miles; 1 mile from Coast Path) – **Swanage** (8 miles) – Studland (5 miles; Studland is located 2 miles before the Path's end at Sandbanks)

<u>Top attractions</u>: Lyme Regis and nearby Charmouth have museums featuring local history and geology. It is possible to go fossil hunting on the coast between these towns with a good chance of success.

Fishing boats in the harbor at West Bay.

East of Lyme Regis Golden Cap Estate has about ten miles of trails in fields and woods. West of Lyme Regis Undercliffs Reserve has thick woods and points of geological interest.

The Swannery in Abbotsbury is home to over 1,400 wild swans. There are other attractions in this beautiful village.

About four miles inland from Swanage the magnificent ruins of Corfe Castle command a hilltop. Visitors can reach the castle by road, steam engine railway, or open ridgeline trail.

The Coast Path circles the Isle of Portland (page 95), which has a Mediterranean feeling, superb views, and interesting sights. The Isle lies south of Weymouth and west of Osmington Mills.

Circle walks, in addition to the Isle of Portland, are at Sidmouth, Abbotsbury, Osmington Mills, Kimmeridge, Kingston, Swanage, and Studland.

RECOMMENDED LODGING

A good way for a hotel or B & B to be included on this list was to have a vacancy when we called as we walked the Path. In addition, during a 2003 auto tour we evaluated many places suggested by other travelers and other sources. We enjoyed and highly recommend the places we list.

The criteria for recommendation include view and location, comforts, food, welcome and care, ambiance, and historic interest.

If a village is listed in a section in the previous pages, but is not here, the SWCP Guide will have low-to-medium priced lodging listed that other hikers have recommended. The Guide is an excellent source for over 800 B & Bs, some in villages not mentioned in this book.

If the lodging is upscale ("upmarket" in England), we say so. In June, 2003 upscale lodging generally cost at least £35 ($56.00) per person.

Phone numbers for all recommended lodgings are given.

SECTION ONE
Countisbury: Coombe Farm 01598 41236
Ilfracombe: Varley House 01271 863927
Isle of Lundy: book lodging through Landmark Trust 01237 470422
Lee: Lee Bay Hotel 01271 867600 upscale
Lynmouth: Rising Sun Hotel 01598 753328 upscale

In 1690 a gambler used his winnings to build the Pack o' Cards in Combe Martin. Each level of this pub, which offers accommodations, supports a smaller level, 4 floors, 13 rooms, and 52 windows in all.

At the Pack there is a brutal quiz show once a week for the patrons, as is the custom in some pubs.

The Pack is a vibrant place that adults with children might want to see before reserving rooms.

THE SHOWER

We are spending the night in a pub that has an unusual phone. It sucks money and shuts down after every ten seconds of conversation.

This evening I strip down for a hot shower and discover the water is freezing. I need a shower because I have just returned from running.

I turn the knob to a 9. I turn it to a 1. I turn it back and forth, waiting a good long wait after each turn to give the water a fair chance to warm up. I push it. I pull it. I give up.

I have three choices.

1. Peter is due back. I can wait for him and send him to get help.
2. I can put my sweaty clothes back on and go get help myself.
3. I can fill the sink and take what I call a sponge bath.

After draining the sink and dressing, I head downstairs half clean and slightly itchy.

In the softest tone possible, I politely suggest to the bartender, our host, that his shower might be broken.

"Oh?" he says. "We haven't had any complaints with it, but I'll go take a look."

Making light of the situation, I suggest with a slight laugh that maybe his customers have been too polite to say anything.

"Not <u>his</u> customers," a bloke at the bar says.

The bar patrons are getting involved.

"Did you pull the cord to turn it on?" one of them asks, just to rule out the ultimate stupidity.

"Cord?"

"Outside the shower box. It turns on the power."

"I think I can handle this," I say to our host.

The rest of the evening goes smoothly. We don't need to make any more phone calls.

- Steve

IN THE DARK

As we leave our B & B to go out for dinner, the owner asks us to enter quietly on our return.

Do we look like gorillas? Of course, we will enter quietly.

We slip in around 9:30 PM and at a reasonable hour prepare for bed.

Steve is about to use the bathroom, so I decide to use one across the hall that the owner had let me use after the fuse blew earlier that evening.

The hallway is black. There are stairs leading down to a landing and back up to the bathroom. The light switch, which I grope for, is on the far wall. I forget about the stairs.

My 215 pounds fall on the landing like a boulder. The house shakes.

The owner charges out of his bedroom in his pajamas trying to yell at me in a whisper.

"Don't you realize there are other guests? Didn't I tell you to be quiet? Haven't you any courtesy?" And so on.

I return to our room, abashed.

I am sitting on my bed in the new quiet when there is a loud banging on the door. We hear a muffled outcry from the lady of the house, who says, "Would you please turn off that bathroom light? The entire house is humming."

It seems a generator kicks in when the bathroom light is on.

Steve finishes his business in the dark.

The next morning we go down to breakfast eager to find out what the owners will say.

They say, "Tea or coffee?"

- Peter

Left, at Exmoor Falconry & Animal Farm, where a falconer shows his birds of prey at no charge.

Lynmouth: The Tors Hotel 01598 753236
Lynton: Highcliff House Hotel 01598 752235 upscale
        St. Vincent House Hotel 01598 752244
        Sinai House 01598 753227
        Woodlands 01598 752324
Minehead: Kenella House 01643 703128
        The Old Ship Aground 01643 702087
Mortehoe: Rockleigh House 01271 870704
Porlock Weir: The Anchor Hotel & Ship Inn 01643 862753
        Andrews on the Weir 01643 863300 standard and upscale
        Porlock Vale House 01643 862338 very upscale
Silcombe: Silcombe Farm 01643 862248
West Lynch: Exmoor Falconry & Animal Farm 01643 862816
Woolacombe: Watersweet Hotel 01271 870333 very upscale

SECTION TWO
Boscastle: The Old Coach House 01840 250398
        Trerosewill Farm 01840 250545
        The Wellington Hotel 01840 250202 upscale
Bossiney: Bossiney House Hotel 01840 770240

The Treyarnon Waterbeach Hotel has a rough putting course on its lawn.

Bossiney: Willapark Manor Hotel 01840 770782 standard and upscale
Buck's Mills: The Old Mill 01237 431701
Bude: The Edgcumbe Hotel 01288 353846
        The Falcon Hotel 01288 352005 upscale
Clovelly: 55 The Quay 01237 431436
        The Red Lion Hotel 01237 431237 upscale
Constantine Bay: Treglos Hotel 01841 520727 very upscale
Crackington Haven: Coombe Barton Inn 01840 230345
        Trevigue 01840 230418
Hartland Quay: Hartland Quay Hotel 01237 441218
Morwenstow: Cornakey Farm 01288 331260
        Old Vicarage 01288 331369
Newquay: The Corisande Manor Hotel 01637 872042 upscale
        Salty Towers 01637 859112
Padstow: Seafood Restaurant & St. Petrocs 01841 532700 very upscale
        Port Isaac: Slipway Hotel 01208 880264
Portgaverne: Headlands 01208 880260 standard and upscale
        The Port Gaverne Hotel 01208 880244 upscale
Trebarwith: The Mill House Inn 01840 770200 standard and upscale
Treyarnon: The Waterbeach Hotel 01841 520292 upscale

SECTION THREE
Botallack: Manor Farm 01736 788525
Cubert: Sunnycot 01637 830353
Hayle: Beckside Cottage 01736 756751
Land's End: Land's End Hotel 01736 871844 upscale
Perranporth: Cellar Cove Hotel 01872 572110
Porthcurno: Mariner's Lodge 01736 810236
       Sea View House 01736 810638
Portreath: Cliff House 01209 842008
Sennen: Old Success Inn 01736 871232 upscale
St. Agnes: Driftwood Spars Hotel 01872 552428
St. Ives: Garrack Hotel 01736 796199 upscale
       Michaelmas Cottage 01736 798086
Treen: Cove Cottage 01736 798317 upscale
       Gurnard's Head Hotel 01736 796928
Zennor: Trewey Farm 01736 796936

Below, the 1681 Manor Farm in Botallack has narrow stairs, a dark paneled dining room, and a very fine breakfast. John Wesley preached here.

SECTION FOUR
Cadgwith: Mengarth 01326 290794
Church Cove: Landewednack House 01326 2290909 upscale
Coverack: The Bay Hotel 01326 280464 upscale
        The Croft 01326 280387
Falmouth: The Falmouth Hotel 08000 193121 upscale
        The Home Country House Hotel 01326 250427
Gillan: Tregildry Hotel 01326 231378 very upscale
Gunwalloe: Halzephron Inn 01326 240406 upscale
Helford: Lean Farmhouse 01326 231022 upscale
        Point 01326 231666
Housel Bay: Housel Bay Hotel 01326 290417 upscale
Lamorna: Lamorna Cove Hotel 01736 731411 very upscale
Mawnan Smith: Budock Vean Hotel 01326 252100 very upscale
Marazion: Mount Haven Hotel 01736 710249 upscale
Mousehole: Thatched Cottage 01736 731333
        Ship Inn 01736 731234
Mullion Cove: Mullion Cove Hotel 01326 240328 very upscale
        Ridgeback Lodge Hotel 01326 280258
Newlyn: Harbour Heights 01736 350976
Porthallow: Valley View House 01326 280370

Penzance: Chy-an-Mor 01736 363441
        Penzance Arts Club 01736 363761 upscale
        The Summer House Restaurant 01736 363744 upscale
        Yacht Inn 01736 362787
Porthleven: Anchor Cottage 01326 574391
        Harbor Inn 01326 573876 upscale
        St. Loy Cove: Cove Cottage 01736 810010 upscale
Ruan Minor: New Thatch 01326 290257

SECTION FIVE

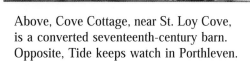

Carlyon Bay: The Carlyon Bay
    Hotel 01726 812304
    very upscale
Cawsand/Kingsand: Avon House
    01752 822229
    Cliff House 01752 823110
    The Halfway House Inn
      01752 822279 upscale
Charlestown: Ardenconnel 01726
    75469

Above, Cove Cottage, near St. Loy Cove,
is a converted seventeenth-century barn.
Opposite, Tide keeps watch in Porthleven.

    Pier House Hotel 01726 67955 upscale
    T'Gallants 01726 70203
Fowey: The Fowey Hotel 01726 832551 very upscale
    The Galleon Inn 01726 833014
    Marina Hotel 01726 833315 very upscale
Gorran Haven: Llawnroc Inn 01726 843461 standard and upscale
    Piggy's Pantry 01726 843545
Looe: The Old Bridge House 01503 263159
    Hannafore Point Hotel 01503 263273 very upscale
Between Looe and Polperro: Talland Bay Hotel 01503 272667 very upscale
Lower Tregantle: Fir Cottage 01752 822626
Mevagissey: Mevagissey House 01726 842427
    Travalsa Court Hotel 01726 842468
Par: Polbrean House 01726 812530
Pendower: Crugsillick Manor 01872 501214 upscale
    Pendower Beach House & Hotel 01872 501257 upscale
Plymouth: The Duke of Cornwall Hotel 01752 275850 very upscale
Polperro: Crumplehorn Inn 01503 272348
    The Watchers 01503 272296
Polruan: Quayside House 01726 870377
Portscatho: Hillside House 01872 580526
Portloe: Fuglers 01872 501482
    The Lugger Hotel 01872 501322 very upscale
    The Tregain 01872 501252
St. Mawes: The St. Mawes Hotel 01326 270266 upscale

The Smugglers Inn in Osmington Mills housed some nefarious guests, including Pierre Latour, aka French Peter. Lodgers have to accept second billing in this busy establishment, but the thirteenth-century atmosphere makes up for any neglect.

SECTION SIX

Beesands/Beeson: Marybank 01548 580531
Bigbury-on-Sea: Burgh Island Hotel 01548 810514 very upscale
     Warren Point 01548 810616
Brixham: The Berry Head Hotel 01803 853225 upscale
     Harbour View Hotel 01803 853052
Dartmouth: Royal Castle Hotel 01803 833033 very upscale
Hope Cove: The Sand Pebbles Hotel 01548 561673
Maidencombe: Dartmoor Maiden Hotel 01803 328760
     Suite Dreams Hotel 01803 313900
Newton Ferrers: Wood Cottage 01752 872372
River Erme: Windlestraw 01752 698384
Rudder Cove: Gara Rock Hotel 01548 842342
Salcombe: Lyndhurst Hotel 01548 842481
     Menzies Marine Hotel 01332 513330 very upscale
Soar: Soar Mill Cove Hotel 01548 561566 upscale
Start Point: Down Farm 01548 511234
Thurlestone: Thurlestone Hotel 01548 560382 upscale
Torcross: Sea Breeze Cottage 01548 580697
Torquay: Fairmount House Hotel 01803 605446
     Mulberry House 01803 213639
     Osborne Hotel 01803 213311 very upscale

SECTION SEVEN
Axmouth: Dairy Cottage 01297 20366
Branscombe: The Masons Arms 01297 680300 standard and very upscale
Bridport/West Bay: Bramah 01308 456617
        The Purbeck House Hotel 01929 422872 upscale
Kimmeridge/Steeple: Blackmanston Farm 01929 480743
Kingston: Kingston Country Courtyard 01929 481066
Lyme Regis: Cliff Cottage Tea Garden 01297 443334
Osmington Mills: Smuggler's Inn 01305 833125
Seatown: Seahill House 01297 489801 upscale
Sidmouth: The Royal York & Faulkner Hotel 01395 513043 very upscale
Studland: The Manor House 01929 450288 upscale
West Bexington: The Manor Hotel 01308 897616 very upscale
West Lulworth: Gatton House 01929 400252

LODGING TIPS

We generally booked one night ahead and at that time made
arrangements to send our packs before us the next morning.

There were times when we tried four or five B & Bs before we
found a vacancy, and on rare occasions an entire village filled with a
wedding party. Accommodations can be hard to find in the summer
and on weekends, especially in popular destinations. Some villages have
few places of lodging.

Some accommodations are unlisted, so ask for these if desperate.
Tourist Information Centres might find lodging for you while you go shopping.

Note the list of over 800 member-submitted accommodations in the
SWCP Guide. The list specifies en suite (private bathroom), car parking,
dogs welcome, kit transfer, approximate costs, and more.

If television is important to you, ask the B & B if it's available. Ask
for a sea view.

B & Bs tend to be cheaper than hotels, and their intimacy and charm
appealed to us. Prices can go up in the midsummer months. In 2003 we generally
paid about £25.00 to £32.00 per night per person for an en suite room with two
twin beds. The pound was worth about $1.60.

Many B & Bs require cash. Don't expect an ATM in every village.

RECOMMENDED DINING

With apologies to hundreds of fine restaurants, we offer the list below based primarily on our own limited experience. We include the pubs for their wonderful ambiance. The food in those pubs is good enough or better. We generally were frugal in our dining adventures, but sometimes went first class at restaurants noted as "upscale." You might need to reserve more than a day in advance at those establishments.

Section One: Lynton - Mad Hatters; Mortehoe - Rockleigh House; Porlock - Piggy in the Middle; Woolacombe - Watersweet Hotel (upscale)

Section Two: Bude - Villa Restaurant (upscale); Clovelly - The Red Lion; Holywell - Treguth Inn (pub); Morwenstow - The Bush Inn (pub); Newquay - Consande Manor Hotel (upscale); Newquay - Harvest House (pub); Padstow - Seafood Restaurant (upscale); Port Isaac - Golden Lion Inn (pub)

Section Three: <u>Botallack</u> - Queens Arms (pub); <u>Perranporth</u> - The Baywatch; <u>Porthcurno</u> - Logan Rock Inn (pub); <u>Portreath</u> - Tabb's; <u>St. Ives</u> - Alba; <u>St. Ives</u> - Garrack Hotel; <u>St. Ives</u> - Hunter's Lodge; <u>St. Ives</u> - Pig 'n Fish; <u>Treen</u> - Gurnard's Head Hotel; <u>Zennor</u> - Tinner's Arms (pub)

Section Four: <u>Coverack</u> - The Bay Hotel; <u>Falmouth</u> - The Pipe (pub); <u>Falmouth</u> - The Seafood Bar; <u>Gunwalloe Cove</u> - Halzephron Inn (pub); <u>Helford Passage</u> - Ferryboat Inn (pub); <u>Lamorna</u> - Lamorna Cove Hotel (upscale); <u>Lamorna</u> - The Wink Inn (pub); <u>Marazion</u> - The Haven Mount; <u>Mousehole</u> - Cornish Range; <u>Mullion</u> - Ridgeback Lodge Hotel; <u>Perranuthnoe</u> - Victory Inn; <u>Porthallow</u> - The Five Pilchards; <u>Porthleven</u> - Critchard's Seafood Restaurant; <u>St. Loy Cove</u> - Cove Cottage Tea House

Section Five: <u>Cawsand</u> - The Galleon; <u>Fowey</u> - The Lugger; <u>Fowey</u> - Sam's Other Place; <u>Fowey</u> - The Ship Inn (pub); <u>Mevagissey</u> - The Ship Inn (pub); <u>Plymouth</u> - Chez Nous; <u>Polperro</u> - The Bateson's; <u>Polperro</u> - Couch's Brasserie; <u>Portscatho</u> - Plume of Feathers; <u>Portloe</u> - The Ship Inn

Section Six: <u>Beesands</u> - The Cricket Inn; <u>Bigbury-on-Sea</u> - The Cafe; <u>Brixham</u> - The Armada; <u>Dartmouth</u> - Carved Angel (upscale); <u>Dartmouth</u> - The Family Station Restaurant; <u>Salcombe</u> - Catch 55; <u>Soar</u> - Soar Mill Cove Hotel (upscale); <u>Torquay</u> - Number 7 Fish Bistro (upscale)

Section Seven: <u>Lyme Regis</u> - The Fish Restaurant; <u>Swanage</u> - Cauldron Bistro; <u>Swanage</u> - Mama's; <u>Swanage</u> - Mowlem's; <u>West Bay</u> - Riverside; <u>West Bexington</u> - Manor Hotel; <u>West Lulworth</u> - Lulworth Cove Hotel

Left, in Perranporth The Baywatch is the relaxed hot spot on the beach.
Opposite, the chef at The Fish Restaurant in Lyme Regis explains the dishes he can create from his selection of fresh fish.

OGGY OGGY AND A RUBBER DINGHY

Before leaving Falmouth we stop at the Oggy Oggy Pasty Co. Coffee Shop and purchase a pasty, the pastry pouch that contains a moist meat, potato, and vegetable mix.

We carry our heavy packs this morning onto the ferry to St. Mawes, where we will catch a second ferry to Place and there meet the day's taxi.

As we approach St. Mawes, the first mate advises us that the second leg of our water hop has hit a snag. The boat used for that crossing is in dry dock under repair. Before we panic, he spots a friend in a rubber dinghy and persuades him to give us a ride.

We board the tipsy dinghy and search with some concern for any possible landing site. There is none. When the time comes to disembark, we go overboard into water up to our waists and wade ashore.

We reach dry land without a slip. We see a red MG, our taxi, waiting for us on schedule. We say good-by to our heavy packs, put on our light packs, and begin the day's hike, happy that good luck has overcome the bad. At lunch time we each enjoy an Oggy Oggy pasty.

FOOD TIPS

– Devon specialties will help you put on the extra pounds you need for your upcoming Arctic exploration. Try the fudge, the clotted cream with jam on scones, and the pasties, which are lighter, if the word can apply, when created at a bakery or restaurant.

Above, Steve relaxes in Combe Barton. Opposite, the Oggy Oggy Pasty Shop in Falmouth.

– A pudding is a dessert. A biscuit is a cookie. A custard … just figure that English dessert names have nothing to do with the American language.

– Unless you feel like a rabbit, ask for salad dressing.

– Cider is as alcoholic as beer. We like it.

– Expect breakfast to be served from 8:30 to 9:30.

– The arterial damage from one serving of fried bread is equal to that from an intravenous feeding of five Big Macs. Since leaving a pile of fried bread on your plate is not polite, you might request no fried bread. You could skip half of the "full breakfast" and not go hungry.

– Don't miss the experience of having dinner at a pub (short for Public House). Pubs have atmosphere.

– The standard tip in restaurants is 10%. You don't need to tip for meals ordered at the bar and brought to your table with minimal service.

HISTORY ON THE RUN

Americans descend from Colonial days and 1776. The English descend
from over 2,000 years of history. Are you in need of a brush-up? Here it
comes, with a bias towards southwest England.

As you proceed, remember that English history is about representative
government, exploration, literature and the arts, murder, mayhem,
invasions, internecine warfare, and royalty run amok. We recommend it.

The first invasion in southwest England occurs in about 400,000 BC when
Stone Age humans wander in and attack the local inhabitants, mostly deer,
bear, and woolly mammoths.

A teenager's jawbone dating to about 30,000 BC has been found near
Torquay on Devon's south coast.

After the last ice age, from about 8,000 BC, Mesolithic people in greater
numbers roam a forested land, but by 5,000 BC the land bridge to Europe
is cut, and migration slows.

Left, the Ballowell Barrow at Carn Gloose near St. Just was excavated in Victorian times. A barrow, or tumulus, is a Bronze Age burial site covered by a large mound of earth or stones. Opposite, a tumulus on a high ridge east of Abbotsbury and east of the Hardy Monument.

From about 4,000 BC Neolithic (New Stone Age) settlers arrive from the Atlantic coast of Europe. They grow crops and raise sheep and cattle. They have tombs, called quoits in some places and cromlechs in others, which have massive stone slabs for roofs.

From about 2,000 BC the Beaker Folk, named for their pottery, arrive from Europe. They hunt and fight with bows and arrows. They work in metals. They erect massive stone circles and use burial mounds called barrows. In the time of the Beaker Folk the Bronze Age begins. Using bronze, an alloy of copper and tin, people improve their tools and weapons. From about 1,500 BC the people of Cornwall send tin in trade to Ireland and Europe.

Around 600 BC the Celts arrive from Europe with Iron Age technology, leading to further improvements in tools and weapons. If no Beaker Folk are nearby to attack, the clans and kings of the fierce Celts fight each other. They build hill forts and ride horse-drawn chariots. They practice human sacrifice, and they produce beautiful works of art. Trade in tin and bronze products increases. The people of southwest England speak Celtic as their first language for over 2,000 years, into the sixteenth century.

KING ARTHUR SLEPT HERE

Yesterday the vicar at the church in Hennett, near Boscastle, told me, "The church is Norman, but the font is Saxon. Three crosses outside are Celtic."

When he left, I asked his assistant if the roof was the Norman original. "No, no, no," he told me. "No part of the church is Norman."

I asked if the font was Saxon. "No, no, no," he said. "It's more recent than that."

One cross outside was Celtic.

Recently we found the Bronze Age wall carvings in Rocky Valley. The carvings are intricate designs that look like mazes. They date from about 1600 BC, or else from around 200 years ago. Our guidebook is not sure.

Today we are at the site of King Arthur's castle in Tintagel. King Arthur, if he existed, probably lived in the sixth century.

I speak with a uniformed park guide.

"Archeologists used to hate King Arthur," he tells me. "They were spending too much time dealing with a myth. Then last year – do you see that section roped off below? A team of five archeologists last year found what we now call the Arthur stone. Pottery with it dates it to the sixth century."

The stone says, in Latin, PATER COLI AVI FICIT ARTOGNOV.

Translation: Arthur, father of the grandfather of Coll, built this.

The stone is in the Royal Cornwall Museum at Truro.

Peter laughs when I report to him. "No way," he says. "It's too good to be true."

"Oh, yes, the stone," a lady at a National Trust shop says. "King Arthur stopped here on a school bus trip."

So she doesn't think Arthur was there, and neither does Peter, but I want to know, how did the archeologists fake the pottery found with the stone? Five archeologists in on a hoax?

At the site jagged ruins of a castle built around 1230 cling to the cliffs of the high promontory. It's a great place for a castle. I think King Arthur would have loved the view.

- Steve

43 AD – 410 AD: The Romans conquer and rule England. They control Exeter and secure access to the tin mines in Cornwall, but otherwise they have few outposts in southwest England and make little impression on the Celts in that area.

In the fifth century the Angles and Saxons invade England. These people are so fierce, they fight naked. Today the people of England speak Angle-ish. By 600 the Anglo-Saxons have pushed the Celts into Wales and Cornwall. Perhaps King Arthur was a Celtic warlord fighting the Saxons. Conversion of the Celts to Christianity, begun in Roman times, accelerates under the guidance of the "early saints" from Brittany, Ireland and Wales.

The church of St. Nicholas at Studland was built in Saxon and Norman times.

In the eighth century, conversion of the Saxons in Devon begins. St. Boniface (680-754), one of the greatest of English saints, receives his education at a Celtic monastery in Exeter and spreads the faith to the Saxons in Devon.

871-899: Alfred the Great rules. Alfred, a West Saxon, halts an invasion of England by the Vikings from Denmark and shares rule of the land with them. Battles are frequent in the southwest, where Saxons and Celts unite against the Danes.

c. 924 - 940: The reign of King Athelstan. A Saxon, Athelstan conquers the Celts and controls the greater part of England after defeating a league of Welsh, Scots, and Danes. The Celtic culture in southwest England is not changed.

1066: A year to remember. William the Conqueror and the Normans invade England. They never leave. For over 200 years French is the language of the schools and the upper class, though the people of southwest England still speak Celtic. A profitable trade develops between southwest England and France. The English export tin from Cornwall and cloth spun from Devon wool.

In 1086 William's Domesday Book provides England's first census. Cows, sheep, and pigs are counted, but not all people. The book shows a population of 60,000 people in Devon.

1147 and 1190: The second and third crusades depart from Dartmouth.

1215: King John is forced to sign the Magna Carta, giving rights and liberties to his barons and bishops.

From the beginning of the thirteenth century Cornish tin mining accelerates. The Crown grants special privileges to "stannary towns" in Cornwall and Devon where tin is processed. If a tin ingot passes inspection, the official stamps a corner of it. French for the stamp and for the corner is "coin." Tin production reaches its peak in the eighteenth century.

1272-1307: The reign of Edward I, "Longshanks." Edward in 1272 imposes customs duties along the coast. The smuggling that results lasts into the nineteenth century.

1337: Edward III claims the French throne and begins the

Saint Winwaloe Church, between Porthleven and Mullion Cove, mostly fifteenth century.

The toll house at Worthy near Porlock Weir dates to the reign of Edward I in the late thirteenth century.

Hundred Years' War. England invades France repeatedly. Henry V and the English longbows are victorious at Agincourt in 1415. Joan of Arc is burned at the stake in 1431. The French burn Fowey and Looe in Cornwall. Edward makes his son, the Black Prince, the Duke of Cornwall.

1348-1349: The Black Death reaches England. By 1370 the plague has struck most of the towns and villages in southwest England.

1485: Richard III, usurper and the murderer of Edward IV's young sons, is defeated at Bosworth Field by Henry VII, the first Tudor king. Though of Celtic origin, Henry suppresses without mercy a rebellion of 15,000 Cornish protesting his tax levies. Three months later the Cornish rally around Perkins Warbeck, who claims to be one of Edward IV's butchered sons. They are crushed again.

1509-1547: The reign of powerful Henry VIII. When the Pope won't allow him to divorce his first wife, Henry declares himself head of the

William of Orange, in Brixham.

church in England in order to marry his second wife, Anne Boleyn. He later has Anne beheaded in favor of a new wife, the third of a total of six. Henry takes the vast wealth and lands of the church.

In 1549 rebels from Cornwall and Devon lead the "Prayer Book Rebellion" against the law that requires religious services to be conducted in a foreign tongue, English. At this time few people in southwest England can speak or understand English. The rebellion is crushed.

1558-1603: The reign of Elizabeth I. The wily Virgin Queen rules at the height of the Renaissance, in the time of Shakespeare, Drake, and Raleigh. Both Drake and Raleigh are from Devon. The Spanish Armada, first spotted at Lizard Point in Cornwall, or else at St. Michael's Mount, is repulsed off the shores of Cornwall in 1588 and later is half destroyed in a storm. In 1595 Spanish raiders burn the Cornish ports of Mousehole, Newlyn, and Penzance. From this time ships used to fight the Spanish and French sail from Devon ports. Devon farmers provision the ships.

In 1620 the Mayflower leaves from Plymouth.

1642-1660: In England's Civil War Cromwell and the Puritans/Parliamentarians/ Roundheads defeat the Royalists and establish the Commonwealth/Protectorate. Cromwell destroys many treasures of many churches. Charles I, who does not accept defeat gracefully, is beheaded in 1649. Southwest England, generally Royalist, is embroiled in the ebb and flow of battle. Charles II, who flees to France in 1651, resumes the royal line in 1660.

1660-1685: The reign of Charles II. Charles has at least 13 mistresses and at least 14 illegitimate children, but no legal heir.

When Charles' brother James II (1685-1688) favors Catholics, Parliament offers the throne to Holland's William of Orange. William lands in Brixham on Devon's south coast with 600 vessels and 20,000 Dutch and German troops. He is there to save England from the Catholics. The people of Devon rally to his cause. William rules from 1689 to 1702. Religious strife subsides in southwest England.

1760-1820: The reign of George III, who becomes increasingly insane. With the help of the French, the American Colonies gain their independence. The Industrial Revolution is underway.

From 1803 to 1815 the English fight Napoleon. During the war the English gentry forsake their traditional grand tour of Europe and flock to England's south coast.

The Tilly Whim Caves east of Swanage are the remains of eighteenth-century limestone quarries. Tilly was a quarryman who perfected the whim, a makeshift crane that lowered stone to barges waiting below. Workers split the rock with punches, wedges and hammers.

GOD BLESS OUR HOME

This evening a light is on in the castle. The castle crowns St. Michael's Mount, a granite crag risen from the sea off Cornwall's coast.

In the twelfth century Benedictine monks built a priory here. Henry VIII stole the place, and in 1588 English troops on the Mount warned of the approach of the Spanish Armada. The St. Aubyn family has lived here since 1660.

Tonight the Lord and Lady are at home.

"Have you seen my glasses, dear?"

"I think they're in the kitchen. There's some leftover quiche in the fridge."

"Where's the section with the crossword puzzle?"

"I have it. Sweetie, you'd better have John see about the portcullis over the main gate. It's slipping."

This evening a light is on in the castle.

In the 1840's Isambard Kingdom Brunel brings the railway from London to the southwest. The tourist industry thrives in Torquay, Exmouth, and Sidmouth.

1837-1901: The reign of Queen Victoria, longest ruling monarch. The empire is at its height.

June 18, 1940: "Let us therefore brace ourselves to our duties, and so bear ourselves that, if the British Empire and its Commonwealth last for a thousand years, men will still say: 'This was their finest hour.'" - Winston Churchill

In 1941 German air raids level the city of Plymouth.

In 1944 Slapton Sands, a three mile beach on the south coast of Devon, is a major training site for the invasion of Normandy. On June 5 thousands of young British, Americans, and Canadians leave from Cornwall and Devon ports to attack the beaches of Normandy.

1952 - The reign of Queen Elizabeth II.

LOGAN ROCK

South of Porthcurno there is a massive boulder named Logan Rock. Said to weigh 80 tons, the rock balances precariously on a granite precipice.

When a renowned Cornish antiquary of the nineteenth century declared that no mortal could move the rock from its position, his nephew, a lieutenant in the navy, took up the challenge. With the assistance of ten sailors from his revenue cutter, he dislodged the rock.

After a local outcry, the Admiralty ordered him to return the stone to its rightful position. The secretary of the South West Coast Path Association, Eric Wallis, explains how Lieutenant Hugh Colwill Goldsmith put the rock back.

Logan Rock casts its shadow.

"Condemned as a vandal, he promised to have it replaced. Preparations took several months and required blocks, chains, ropes, capstans, and massive wooden shear-legs supplied by the Admiralty.

"Work started on 29 October 1824, and four days later the rock was back in place in front of an audience numbering thousands. The total cost to Lt. Goldsmith was 130 pounds and 8 shillings. The accounts show 13s 6d being paid out to 60 men of St. Just who did very little but drink beer.

"It was a remarkable feat of engineering, but no amount of skill could recreate the precise balance that had made the great stone "log" (rock) so spectacularly.

"The equivalent of 13/6d must be a tidy sum today."

We wonder, was the lieutenant happy to spend his money, having proven his point?

THE PAST

On a flat and windswept field high above the sea Tintagel Church stands firm against the storms. Built in the eleventh and twelfth centuries, it is the oldest church in Cornwall.

A weathered life preserver marks one of the graves in the cemetery. It stands on a cross in memory of a cabin boy who was the sole fatality when his ship was wrecked on the rocks below.

Inside the church a Norman font commemorates the line of the Dukes of Cornwall, who first came to England with William the Conqueror. Tucked into a corner of the transept is a milestone bearing the Latin inscription of Roman Emperor Licinius, who was put to death by rival Emperor Constantine in 324 AD.

Thomas Hardy is said to have stormed out of this church with his second wife when the pastor saw fit in his sermon to lecture Tom about the shabby treatment he had given his first wife.

Old churches gather history.

Left, Wheal Trewavas, Cornish for "mine in the village of Wavas," stands east of Prussia Cove. Below, in Botallack extensive remains of tin and copper operations date from the nineteenth century. Trade in copper and tin dates to the Bronze Age on the coast of Cornwall. Opposite, Tintagel Church.

MINING

Near Botallack we look down a steep grassy slope to where two tin mining towers hug the ledges directly above the roiling sea. Next to these structures an incline shaft long ago was sunk into the sea bottom, providing access to a network of man-made tunnels and caves where the Botallack miners dug their ore.

Walter White, a Coast Path walker in 1854, came to these mines and noted in his journal, "Ever you hear the din of the stampers, the gush of the pumps, the clank of machinery, and the restless wash of the sea below. There are tramways, too, and trains of wagons running to and fro, and men and boys scrambling up and down paths that seem too steep for a goat. ... I had no motive ... to induce me to descend into the darkness, and the foul, heated air of the mine."

WRECKERS

From before the 1500's, men plundered wrecked ships along the Cornish coast. By the 1700's, as the population of Cornwall grew, hundreds and even thousands of people gathered quickly at the site of a wreck to remove all its cargo and sometimes every trace of the ship. Wreckers might arrive before a ship went down to cheer its destruction.

In 1720 a Dutch ship loaded with brandy and saffron ran aground near Falmouth. The wreckers became drunk on the brandy and with a candle set the spirits on fire. The flames consumed the cargo, the ship, and two of the wreckers.

On that occasion the authorities sent seven or eight of the "Country People" to jail as an example, but the warning was not effective. Plundering reached its height later in that century.

There is a story from 1739 that when news of a wreck came to a church, the clergyman pleaded with his congregation to remain seated until he had removed his cassock, "so that we can all start fair."

In 1753 a ship was beached in good condition, the *Sherbourne Mercury* reported, "till a parcel of Cornish Barbarians from St. Agness, Lower St. Columbe, etc., came to the place, and demanded the whole as wreck." A local judge rescued some silk for the owners and was going to have guns fired on the mob to protect the rest of the goods, but the mob attacked him, carried off the rest of the loot, and burned the ship.

Such stories from that time are common. Men, women, and children descended on their prey armed with pick axes, crowbars, and sharp axes, to be used on the ship, its contents, and anyone who opposed the theft. Scenes of rage, drunkenness, fighting, and death ensued. People carried off their booty in kettles and any conveyance possible. It was common for the country people to steal any goods the authorities salvaged for the ship owners. Local gentry often held wrecking rights recognized by the local people.

Even when the wreckers were cooperating with each other, as was normal, wrecking was dangerous work. Ships frequently ran aground at night in pounding surf. They heaved up on rocks at the base of steep cliffs, where swirling eddies were dangerous in daylight and in calm weather, and more so at night in a storm, when wreckers plied their trade by the dim light of lanterns. At Morvah near St. Just a man was swept off Carn Gloose rocks and was lost in front of hundreds of people watching from the top of the cliff. Within a few minutes another took his place. In other cases small boats capsized and the occupants drowned.

At Woolacombe when times were hard, the natives made their living at the business of wrecking. At night they led 6 to 8 donkeys up the hill to Mortehoe with a lantern tied to each donkey's tail. Sailors on a dark sea thought they were seeing lights along the hills encircling Ilfracombe and its harbor. The sailors headed into the nonexistent harbor and ran aground. Not wanting witnesses, the plunderers took no prisoners.

Frederick Farrar in *Early Days of Christianity* (1882) notes that, "The men of Cornwall went straight from church to light their beacon fires."

By the end of the eighteenth century, religious revival and the organization of militia to fend off a Napoleonic invasion dampened wrecking ardor. The plaque below the figurehead of the Cutty Sark at Greenwich notes that the ship was lured ashore by wreckers, with 7 men drowned, 10/23/1842, and adds that the atrocity was "the last known instance of a ship being trapped by wreckers."

In all ages there were people who helped the victims of wrecks. Now almost every village has a rescue squad, and Cornish rescuers have saved hundreds of lives.

Primary source: *Tales of the Cornish Wreckers* by John Vivian.
Additional source: *The Wreckers* by Iain Lawrence.

DOOM BAR

Just opposite Doom Bar at Stepper Point, we meet a Norwegian girl sitting by the side of the trail with a violin case in hand. She offers to play for us, but we tell her we need to move on. We ask ourselves later, have we lost our minds?

Perhaps we fear the curse of Doom Bar. This bar, stretching across the mouth of the Camel Estuary, wrecked over 300 ships between 1760 and 1920. Legend says that a sailor killed a mermaid, thinking her to be a seal, and in retribution she cursed the estuary with the deadly bar. Do we sense that this violin toting maiden is the mermaid?

At Hawker's Cove we ascend to the top of the cliff and circle Stepper Point, noting on the way capstans installed on the lee side of the headland. These are stout poles around which rope tied to a ship could be wrenched by a team of donkeys, so the ship could be warped (pulled) past Doom Bar.

We eat our packed lunches at a cliff edge with seagulls soaring up the rock face in front of us. They dip and dive to the foaming sea below. Steve insists that I move back from the edge of the cliff.

- Peter

Right, Peter has been kind enough to move back from the edge of the cliff at Stepper Point, near Padstow. Opposite, the walls of Culbone Church are twelfth century.

FIVE BITS OF HISTORY

What happened to the spire on the Church of St. Dubricius in Porlock? Some people think that the gale of 1703 blew it over the hill and into the valley of Culbone, where the spire that rests on the smallest parish church in England looks suspiciously as if it belongs on the church in Porlock.

Others believe that the workers hired to build the spire followed the hounds on a hunt that went through town. The workers were never seen again.

If you visit Culbone, you might note that Thomas, chaplain of Cattenor (Culbone) was indicted in 1280, "for that he had struck Albert of Esshe on the head with a hatchet, and so killed him."

Was it hard to find a good chaplain for a church that is five feet wide?

On the side of a hill sloping to the sea, Hawker's Hut was a refuge for the slightly mad Vicar of Morwenstow, who came to the village in 1834. The vicar made his hut from driftwood and used it as a place of meditation. Here he wrote poems and smoked an occasional pipe of opium.

The vicar married a woman 30 years older, and when she died, he married a girl of 17.

He brought to his churchyard the bodies of drowned sailors to give them proper burial.

Buck's Mills is a fishing village 400 years old. A stream runs through the middle of the village under the only street. The stream separates two parishes. Folks on one side of the stream vote in Buck's Mills, but those on the other side vote in a village miles away.

This beacon between Golden Cap and West Bay is a replica of those used centuries ago.

In 1850 at the age of 16 Constance Emily Kent murdered her baby stepbrother. The murder was an act of revenge because her father had married Constance's governess. The infant was the child of Constance's father and the governess.

Constance was in jail for 20 years. After her release, she moved to Melbourne, where she became famous for her nursing work. She was a celebrated centenarian.

The house where Constance lived as a child on a hill above Sidmouth fell into ruin and was demolished in 1930. The lovely formal gardens of the home have been restored. To find them, ask for the Connaught Gardens.

As early as medieval times all along the south coast and then across inland England there were beacons on prominent hills. In the event of possible invasion, the first watch to spot the suspect fleet would light their beacon, day or night. The substances burned included plenty of tar-like material, which gave off black smoke.

Attendants at the next beacon would see the flames or smoke and light theirs, and so on. It took only a few hours for the king or queen in London to be warned of the threat. In this way news of French or Spanish invasion was sent quickly to the Crown.

Lorna Doone country at the Valley of the Rocks.

NONESSENTIALS
LITERARY PLACES

PORLOCK: *Lorna Doone* by Richard Blackmore is set in this area. Near the Valley of the Rocks there is "the hollow strech behind the cliffs," the haunt of the soothsayer, Mother Melldrum. Everyone we met around Porlock had read *Lorna Doone*. It's a classic, but not easy reading.

WOOLACOMBE, and the south coast of Cornwall and Devon in general: *The Wreckers* by Iain Lawrence is a gripping children's book. We recommend it for ages 10 to 14. There are some ghastly details in it. The research is solid.

CORNWALL: *Poldark* and other novels by Winston Graham are filled with Cornish history and portrayals of the old families. The setting for the series is in the area of Perranporth and St. Agnes in the late eighteenth and early nineteenth centuries.

Part of the grounds that became the setting for Daphne DuMaurier's *Rebecca*.

BOSCASTLE: A half-day's walk from Boscastle is the Church of St. Julitta, where Thomas Hardy met and married his first wife, Emma. She inspired his story, *A Pair of Blue Eyes*.

PORT ISAAC TO PADSTOW: The grave of Sir John Betjeman is at St. Enodoc Church, across the River Camel from Padstow. Sir John became Poet Laureate of England in 1972. He wrote often of Cornwall scenes.

GWITHIAN: About two miles north of Gwithian the lighthouse on Godrevy Island is the one in Virginia Woolf's novel, *To the Lighthouse*.

HELFORD: Frenchman's Creek is just outside Helford and is the setting for Daphne DuMaurier's novel by that name.

GRIBBIN HEAD: The Gribbin is near Polkerris, west of Fowey. At the neck of Gribbin Head the Path passes through a park-like setting that inspired Daphne DuMaurier in her novel *Rebecca*. DuMaurier lived nearby in a home called Menabilly that became the fictional Manderley.

LYME REGIS: In the local museum we found information on two novels set in this area: Jane Austen's *Persuasion*, and *The French Lieutenant's Woman* by John Fowles.

FAVORITE EPITAPHS AND MEMORIALS

On a bench in a park above Padstow Harbor, in memory of Tommy Morrisey, Padstow fisherman, 1915 - 1996:

> Just tell me old shipmates
> I'm taking a trip mates
> and I'll see you some day
> in Fiddler's Green

On the daymark guide for ships and boats at Portreath, from "For the Fallen," a poem composed on that spot by Laurence Binyon in 1914:

> They shall not grow old, as we
> That are left grow old.
> Age shall not weary them, nor
> The years condemn.
> At the going down of the sun
> And in the morning
> We shall remember them.

On a tombstone in the yard at Saint Winwaloe Church at Church Cove, near Halzephron Cliff:

> DEAR BETTY
> WENT HOME ON 21.4.98
> THE PARTY'S OVER, BUT
> HER SHOWS WILL LAST
> FOREVER
> SADLY MISSED
> BILL AND THE BOYS
> 7.1.1910 – 21.4.98

On a monument on Black Head, beyond Petewan:

> A. L. Rowse, 1903-97, the voice of Cornwall,
> "the land of my content"

FAVORITE SIGNS

1. After crossing the bridge over the River Tamar at Plymouth, a puzzle for Americans:

    END OF FREE RECOVERY ZONE

    The solution: if your car breaks down before that sign, there is no charge for towing it to a safe location. After that sign, you're on your own.

2. On a hillside beyond Marazion, soon after taking a side path up the hill, we pass a discreet "Private" sign, but we don't turn back until the sign that says,

    EVEN MORE PRIVATE

3. At the entrance to a private road beyond Porthleven:

    FREE RANGE CHILDREN ON COASTAL FOOTPATH

4. On a table with plants for sale, where you help yourself and put the cost of your purchase in a box:

    STOLEN PLANTS DIE

5. Near the Valley of the Rocks, in the middle of a pasture:

    On this spot
    1st April 1780
    nothing happened

Above, the perambulators, Peter and Jean, are on the right. The village of Morwenstow is in the background. Opposite, a sign near Morwenstow protects a private path.

NOTES ON A FOREIGN LAND

At Morwenstow we have drinks at the pub with Peter and Jean, about our ages but twice as fit. They recently finished their annual Perambulation of Exmoor Forest, 32 miles around in one day. The excursion is also called "beating the boundaries" and is a historic activity.

Many people we meet on the Path are over 70, but usually they don't go much faster than we do.

On the way to Port Isaac we stop for refreshments in Trebarwith Strand, a tiny harbor town. A man clad in shorts and an orange waistcoat trots by spearing litter with a pointed stick. Steve, during his early morning jog, spotted the man in Tintagel performing at the same frenetic pace.

The spearsman explains, somewhat breathlessly, that several of the villages in the area employ him to pick up litter and that day he has only half a day to perform a full day's job. He has to pick up his son at school early that afternoon. Where the man has been, the streets are clean.

The British caravans (RVs) are small. The lawns they possess are smaller. A gentleman we speak with as we pass through the caravan park near Budleigh Salterton estimates 5,000 caravans on that site.

"Horrible!" some walkers exclaim, but caravan lots beat 5,000 homes on the coast. The coast and the rural areas inland are protected by strict regulations governing any construction.

On the ferry to Exmouth we speak with a gentle elderly couple. Because we have heavy packs with us, they insist that they will give us a ride to our hotel.

Our conversation is light and full of English humor. We mention the English joy over the French loss in the World Cup match, and we wonder why there is such enmity between the two countries.

The old man's voice hardens. "The arrogant pigheaded French," he says. The diatribe that follows covers the period from 1930 to the present.

Charles DeGaulle is alive and well.

For four dollars per person we catch a morning bus from Osmington Mills to West Lulworth. It is a pleasant ride, but we share the bus with only one other passenger. The driver tells us that the bus service will be discontinued by the end of the year.

"Our fares don't even pay for the diesel gasoline," he explains. "Everyone now commutes to work by car. The losers are the elderly and walkers like you."

The British are experts at anti-clamor. The noise in restaurants is a rustle of leaves. Villages lie becalmed.

The British love word games. Our English in-law walking with us one afternoon invents a game in which participants act out any word with the syllable "log" in it. His dance to suggest logarithm is exceptional. The limericks on the next page are in large measure his fault.

A caravan park above West Bexington.

There was an old man from Tintagel
Who was remarkably agile -
He made a great jump,
Fell on his rump,
And discovered, alas, he was fragile.

There was a young girl of Lamorna
Wealthy before she was borna –
She grew to love hunting
Clad in nothing but bunting,
Which she lost while rounding a corna.

The lads from the village of Austell
Were known to be horribly hostile –
They hit you with clubs
When you entered their pubs
And were generally ter'bly imposs'le.

A disgusting old fellow from Treen
Tells jokes that are very obscene –
They are crude, they are lewd,
They are frightfully rude –
Praise God, no one knows what they mean.

Above, a boundary line of stones near Land's End, which in Cornish (a Celtic language) is Pedn an Laaz, or "end of earth."
Right, near Porthcurno.
Opposite, top: our friends on a crag viewed from the neck of The Lizard, England's most southerly point.
Opposite, bottom: near Land's End.

CRAGS

Fewer than twenty Celtic words have entered our language. One of these is crag, which became a part of English in the Middle Ages.

Given a fierce, guttural sound, the word "crag" can take us back to a time when screaming warriors in bloody combat attacked and defended rocky hill forts while gulls cried overhead and waves pounded the surf below.

The coast of southwest England is a craggy land.

GUIDEBOOKS AND WEB SITES

The publication date is the year of the last revised edition.

THE ESSENTIAL GUIDE

South West Coast Path Guide. Published by South West Coast Path Association (www.swcp.org.uk). Updated each year. See pages 106 and 143 in this book for descriptions of the SWCP Guide.

OTHER HELPFUL GUIDEBOOKS

A. OVERVIEW GUIDES

Leisure Guide Cornwall and The Isles of Scilly. Published by Ordnance Survey and AA. Updated frequently. Holiday highlights in Cornwall, including 10 circle walks.

Leisure Guide Devon and Exmoor. Published by Ordnance Survey and AA. Updated frequently. Holiday highlights in Devon, including 10 circle walks.

Path Descriptions. Published by South West Coast Path Association. Detailed accounts of all aspects of short sections of the Path, including maps and illustrations. 46 booklets cover the entire Coast Path.

The Rough Guide to Devon and Cornwall by Robert Andrews. Published 2001 by Rough Guides Ltd. (www.roughguides.com). Good overview. Includes accommodations and dining.

The Visitor's Guide to Devon by Brian Le Messurier. Published 1994 by Moorland Publishing Company. Good overview of sites and walks in Devon.

Wild horses between Bude and Crackington Haven.

B. TRAIL GUIDES

National Trail Guide, South West Coast Path, four volumes: Minehead to Padstow, Padstow to Falmouth, Falmouth to Exmouth, and Exmouth to Poole. Published 2001-2002 by Aurum Press (tel: 020 7637 3225). Contain sections of Ordnance Survey maps showing details a mile or more inland. Have detailed trail descriptions and a great deal of history. Include circle walks along the Coast Path.

Ordnance Survey Maps. Though not technically trail guides, these maps are some hikers' second most important aid, after the SWCP Guide. Check SWCP Guide for correct series. Order Ordnance maps through www.standfords.co.uk.

Circular Coast Walks Cornwall by Chris Adams. Published 1999 by The Moor, Dale and Mountain Press. Sparse, but to the point, descriptions of 33 walks.

Southwest of Port Isaac.

Circular North Devon Walks by Chris Adams. Published 1998 by the Moor, Dale and Mountain Press. Includes 16 walks along the Coast Path.

Classic Walks: Cornwall. Published 1998 by Norton Publishing Limited (tel: 07000 782688). 60 circle routes, including 41 that involve the Coast Path.

Jarrold Short Walks, Leisure Walks for All Ages. Published by Jarrold Publishing. For the full series: www.totalwalking.co.uk. Include many circle walks that involve the Coast Path.

A companion to the Jarrold Short Walks series: *Pathfinder Guides.* Published 1996 and later by Jarrold Publishing and Ordnance Survey. These three titles have Coast Path walks:

> *Pathfinder Guide Cornwall*
> *Pathfinder Guide Dorset*
> *Pathfinder Guide South Devon and Dartmoor*

Pub Walks Along the Cornwall Coast Path by Eleanor Smith. Published 1997 by Countryside Books. Twenty circular coastal walks.

The South West Coast Path by Paddy Dillon. Published 2003 by Cicerone. Concise pocket-size guidebook with 88 photos and small sections of Ordnance Survey maps. www.cicerone.co.uk.

Walk the Cornish Coastal Path by John H. N. Mason. Published 1999 by Collins. Mapped Guide full of information, including accommodations and pubs. Web site: www.fireandwater.com.

Walks in Historic Devon by Michael Bennie. Published 2001. Includes several Coast Path walks steeped in history.

C. LODGING, SELF-CATERING, AND DINING GUIDES

AA Bed & Breakfast Guide. Published by AA Publishing. Updated each year.

Alastair Sawday's Special Places to Stay:
British Bed & Breakfast
British Hotels, Inns and Other Places
Other titles: www.specialplacestostay.com.
Updated frequently. Include a good number of places in Coast Path villages. Alastair Sawday has a loyal readership.

The Best Bed & Breakfast England, Scotland and Wales. Published by U.K.H.M. Publishing. Updated each year. Descriptions of country houses, town houses, city apartments, manor houses, village cottages, farmhouses, and castles.

English Country Cottages. Published by British Travel International. Updated each year. U.S. tel: 1-800-327-6097. Catalogue of self-catering accommodations.

Staying Off the Beaten Path. Published by Arrow Books. Updated each year. Descriptions of guest houses, small hotels, farms and country houses, all moderately priced.

WEB SITES

A. ORGANIZATIONS

South West Coast Path Association: www.swcp.org.uk; e-mail at
    info@swcp.org.uk
Cornwall Bird Watching and Preservation Society: a Web search will find
    this organization.
Countryside Agency: www.countryside.gov.uk
Devon Bird Watching and Preservation Society: a Web search will find this
    organization.
English Trust: www.english-heritage.org.uk
The National Trust: www.nationaltrust.org.uk
The Ramblers Association: www.ramblers.org.uk
Tourist Information Centres: www.britainexpress.com/TIC/england.htm
        Any TIC will give information on local circle walks, attractions,
and lodging, including self-catering cottages. They will mail some information.
Some have their own Web sites.

B. REGIONS

Cornwall: www.chycar.co.uk
    www.cornwalltouristboard.co.uk
    www.cornish-riviera.co.uk
    www.cornishlight.freeserve.co.uk
Devon: www.devon-connect.co.uk
North Cornwall: www.northcornwall-live.com
South Coast of East Devon and Dorset: www.jurassiccoast.com
Southeast Cornwall: www.southeastcornwall.co.uk
Southwest England: www.englandswestcountry.worldweb.com
Southwest England: www.westcountrynow.com
West Cornwall: www.enjoy-cornwall.co.uk
    www.west-cornwall-tourism.co.uk
West Dorset: www.westdorset.com

North of Port Isaac.

C. COMMUNITIES

Some communities have their own Web sites. For example:
Abbotsbury: www.abbotsbury-tourism.co.uk
Boscastle/Tintagel: www.tintagelweb.co.uk
Dartmouth: www.dartmouth-information.co.uk
Falmouth: www.falmouth-sw-cornwall.co.uk
Fowey: www.fowey.co.uk
Lyme Regis: www.lymeregis.com
Mevagissey: www.mevagissey-cornwall.co.uk
Newquay: www.newquay.org.uk
Plymouth: www.plymouthcity.co.uk
Padstow: www.padstow-cornwall.co.uk
St. Austell: www.cornish-riviera.co.uk

St. Mawes: www.roselandinfo.com
Seaton: www.eastdevon.net/tourism/seaton
Swanage: www.swanage.gov.uk
Torbay: www.torbay.gov.uk
Weymouth: www.weymouth.gov.uk
        A Web search gives information about many other towns on the Coast
Path.

D. LODGING, SELF-CATERING COTTAGES, AND DINING

Classic Cottages: www.classic.co.uk
Cornish Cottages: www.cornishcottageholidays.co.uk
Cornish Farm Holiday: www.cornish-farms.co.uk
Cornwall Accommodations, Restaurants, and Attractions:
    www.kingharryscornwall.co.uk
English Country Cottages: www.britishtravel.com
Resorts and Restaurants: www.resort-guide.co.uk

E. ATTRACTIONS

The Eden Project botanical gardens: www.edenproject.com. The gardens
    are 4 miles east of St. Austell, a short car ride from Mevagissey or
    Fowey. Expect large crowds.
The Minack Theatre (page 123): www.minack.com
The National Maritime Museum (page 127): www.nmmc.co.uk
Trebah Gardens (page 127): www.trebah-garden.co.uk
        A Web search gives information about many other attractions
mentioned in this book. For example:
    Blue Hills Tin Streams (page 123)
    Cockington (page 130)
    Coleton Fishacre Gardens (page 130)
    Hartland Abbey (page 120)
    Lundy Island (page 119)
    Pilchard Works (page 126)
    St. Michael's Mount (page 126)

Southwest of Port Isaac.

F. *A COASTAL AFFAIR*

Gluttons for detail can order a copy of Peter's journal through our Web site, www.walkenglandbooks.com. Peter kept the journal during the five years of the hike. The Web site also has information on how to order *A Coastal Affair* on-line or by snail mail. There is a small charge for the journal.

INDEX

Thanks to the South West Coast Path Association for the photos on pages 23 (Instow), 51 (the Minack Theatre), and 89 (Landslip). Thanks to that organization also for their map of Southwest England that we have adapted for use in this book. Thanks to Roland Barkas and kind strangers for photos in which the authors appear together. The cover photo is from the Andrew Besley photo library (bes.pix@btinternet.com). All other photos in *A Coastal Affair* were taken by the authors.
Photo, opposite: at Land's End.